C0-ATV-677

BEING THE COMMUNITY OF CHRISTIAN LOVE

R. EUGENE STERNER

THE WARNER PRESS
ANDERSON, INDIANA

PRINTED IN THE UNITED STATES OF AMERICA

Contents

Introduction

To think *theologically* about life. That is our assignment. How do we do this? What does it mean?

Theology, of course, is the study about God, who he is and how he relates to his creation and to his people. To think theologically is to think of life in terms of God's purpose and his self-disclosure through the law, the prophets, and history, but most of all through Jesus Christ his Son. It is also to think of God in the only terms we can know—through life, as he has revealed himself in life. To think theologically is to think in a different frame of reference from that to which we are so accustomed, and perhaps well-nigh enslaved.

But our concern is more than thinking only. We are concerned about acting, doing, and being. We are concerned with *responding to God* within life, as his people, seeking to cooperate intelligently and joyously with him in what he is doing in reference to life and people. We are also concerned to *respond to other people* as they live and struggle, to their needs and in terms of what God has done and is now doing.

We assume that God has not abdicated, that he is indeed alive and active, still engaged in his creative work. We assume that, after all we might say about the human predicament, the creation does make sense and God is on his throne. We believe that there is a goal toward which the whole creation moves and that goal is good. This is hope, not wishful thinking but hope in its biblical sense. We know that "somewhere Someone is not stupid."

To think theologically is to think in terms of the God of all history who has a strategy within history and a goal beyond history. Thus life has meaning. We sense the mood and share the viewpoint of Jesus, "My Father works unceasingly, and so do I" (John 5:17, Weymouth).

Christians, as individuals and in their corporate life of fellowship in Christ, have a part in carrying forward Christ's purpose under his lordship. They are to be a responsive and responsible people. When we see the church in this light—as people on mission, ministering people, those engaged in reconciliation—then we see it more clearly. For its nature and its mission are the inseparable two sides of the same coin. The church *is* Christ's continuing redemptive work in the world, through his people. It is not difficult to see why unity among Christians is so important, why we should be of one mind and spirit, rising above petty, partisan concerns and responding to God in what he is doing. Christ is Savior and Lord. That is an accomplished fact and reality, and the church is the unique scene of his lordship.

Admittedly this is idealistic. When we look about us at the organized church as it now is, we are often disappointed. There's the catch! Can we accept the church's essential nature by faith and also work toward the full realization of it? Can we live in the tension of contrast between that which is and that which should be? It is painfully true that the present-day church is not all it should be. It is also true, however, that there is a yeast of new life evident in many quarters.

If we are to respond to human need, we need some understanding of the human predicament, of man's alienation from God, his estrangement from his fellowman, his own condition of guilt and dividedness. Our concern is the sin condition as well as the specific sins, the rebelliousness which is the root cause of evils in society as well as the social conditions which aggravate the existing problem of sin in the human heart. The gospel speaks to the entire human predicament, to a man personally and to men in their life together. The church is intended to be, under God, the object lesson in human brotherhood, the dynamic minority in the midst of the majority, the nucleus of a new order. But we in the church also are human beings with human error and failings.

It is wholesome to remember that the only true and full expression of the will of God among men was in Jesus Christ. The church, even at its best, is but an approximation. Therefore, at the heart and head of the church stands Jesus Christ who has promised to be with us always. His righteousness constantly judges our conduct. His perfect goodness puts to shame our fragmentary goodness. His spirit corrects our spirits. His revelation disciplines our thinking. It is his living presence which makes the true church. Gathered people do not necessarily comprise the church, even though they meet in a churchly edifice. The church is where even two or three are gathered together— wherever it may be—in *his name* (in tune with his purpose and his spirit). It is a condition of relatedness in the life and spirit of Christ. It is a condition of obedience and response to Christ. The church does not stand alone; it stands in Christ. As we seek to know the church as a responsive and responding people, this relationship *in Christ* is fundamental to our understanding.

We seek New Testament meanings and relationships rather than patterns of organization or method. The early Christians seem to have adapted themselves quickly to the varied conditions in different places. They were not, to use J. B. Phillips' graphic phrase, "musclebound by over-organization" nor were they bound to tradition. They were not following some precedent. They were establishing precedent. There was an astonishing flexibility and life in that young church. They were dominated by a cause, a mission. They were overwhelmed people—bowled over by God's mighty act and living in the ruling presence of the risen Lord.

When we attempt to recapture the genius and power of the New Testament church it is not an effort to return to something old but to something central and basic. (There is nothing more timely than that which is timeless.) In our quest we seek the meanings and power of that divine-human encounter when God invaded human life and experience, first through Christ and, beyond that, through those early followers who went out loving not their own lives but with reckless, joyous abandon, and courage born of living faith, "turned the world upside down."

They did not have money or earthly power, position or status, but they had a new kind of power. And as for influence, people were afraid to join them unless they, too, had been radically changed. "None of the rest dared join them, but the people held them in high honor" (Acts 5:13).

They were not the privileged people of the community, the people of status and position. They were common, ordinary people—fishermen, tax collectors, and other unlettered laymen, often despised. But there was a new quality in their lives. Not many noble, not many wise or intellectual people were called—just ordinary people who would dare to obey. It was a remarkable phenomenon that history shifted gears in their time.

Our purpose, then, is to think in terms of what God has done and is now doing. Where is he at work today? Do we dare to assume that he is moving in present-day life and experience? If he is at work, can we be counted on to respond to his call?

Chapter 1

Loneliness Is an Epidemic

It has been said that loneliness is the central sickness of our time. How can the church relate helpfully to this need?

Loneliness? Yes, but not the temporary feeling you get when you are away from your loved ones for a time, not the pain of separation from one who loves you. The loneliness of our time is the deep, restless feeling that no one really cares very much. It is the lack of relatedness, the feeling of standing alone, isolated, without any genuine companionship or understanding. It is that bottled up feeling of never being able to unburden yourself to another, that no one has time or inclination to listen and to hear you through and that, even if someone did hear you, he wouldn't understand. It is the feeling that if people really knew you they wouldn't like you or have any respect for you. It is the lack of real communication with other people.

People wear masks to hide who and what they really are; probably not because they wish to be dishonest, but because they are afraid to be known. We all know what this is like for all of us have done it to some degree. How we have longed for a friend to whom we could fully reveal our thinking, our deep feelings, our dreams and our hopes, our frustrations and defeats, our temptations and our sins, our doubts and fears. But often we do not dare to trust our closest friend with such secrets. One man said, "My life has been a closed book." Another said, "I desperately need a place of confession." And another one said, "Even my wife doesn't know what I'm really like. I have never let her know."

To add to this tragedy of loneliness, we often so successfully deny our real feelings to *ourselves* that we lose—or never gain—a realistic and honest view of ourselves. Thus we deceive ourselves and live in a false kind of world, taking refuge in daydreams of imagination which are self-glorifying, self-gratifying, self-pitying, or otherwise self-deceiving. But then the harsh realities of life must come back, and we are less prepared than before to meet them. It seems clear that many serious emotional and mental disorders arise out of this sense of isolation or estrangement from other people and from ourselves.

Fear and guilt resulting from something in your life which you are afraid to have known—even afraid to face frankly yourself—can lead to real trouble. But we are not interested here in the extreme disorders. Leave that to the specialists. What you see in the extreme in serious cases is true in a lesser degree with "normal" people. The extreme cases call for psychiatric treatment, but some simple lessons and an awareness of the love of God could save many of us a great deal of heartache. That's why, as Christians, we need to understand and appreciate the genius of the gospel and the healing power of genuine Christian fellowship. God's love mediated through the deep relatedness of Christian friends who know the meaning of forgiveness can work wonders of healing.

A Special Loneliness

The loneliness we feel today is different and more intense. It is also more dangerous. In the days of the American frontier when people lived miles apart, there was the loneliness of separation from other people by distance.

Now we are surrounded, even crowded, by other people but separated by walls of fear, prejudice, hostility, pride, or just plain indifference and preoccupation with things, money, status, or work.

In frontier days, while separated from neighbors, the family was generally close-knit and did many things together. They worked in the same fields and kitchens, and the long evenings would be spent in family activities and fun. Now, we are crowded into subways or buses, jostled on the streets, or caught in bumper-to-bumper traffic, and when we get home it may be a house where only part of the family is present for the evening meal. It may be to a place where real human relationships are not felt. Home may be only a stopping place. Parents may be too busy to be companions to their children and to each other. There are many people, yes, but little real relatedness and understanding. (The loneliest spot I can remember was on Times Square in New York one evening at the rush hour.)

In earlier days our fathers and grandfathers could find some relief for their kind of loneliness in any opportunity to get together. They had barn raisings and corn huskings. They got together to peel apples and make apple butter. The country funeral was a major social event—at least it was in the hills of Pennsylvania. People came for miles, even those who had no family relationship or personal friendship. They stayed just about all day, going home late to do the chores. But a city minister will conduct more than one funeral where he helps the funeral director and one or two of his assistants to carry the coffin.

Incidentally, it was in those days that the revival meeting was so widely popular as a means of evangelism. It was a social phenomenon. People were eager to be together. They came in droves. Now they seem to stay away in droves. Now there is television at home where millions of people sit enthralled and glued, movies at the theater, and sports. Evangelism today and tomorrow will take account of people where they really live intellectually and emotionally.

To add to the existing loneliness, our eardrums and our eyeballs are assaulted every hour with the clamor of high pressure advertising and flashing neon signs calling for our money, time, loyalty. Everyone wants us to buy something, give to something, go to something, or do something. I think I hear people saying, "Well, who in all this world cares anything for me?" Even the church, in its attempt to reach people, has often employed the same tactics and techniques.

It presents itself as another organization calling for people whom it wants to use. Often, it shows more contrivance than compassion, more social prestige than spiritual power, more concern with statistics than with salvation, more lust for financial "success" than love for persons. Is it any wonder modern man turns away? Through all this maze and confusion the gospel still says, "God loves you." The true church still says, "We love you." The voice of our Lord may be lost in the din and clatter, but it is just that voice of love, so often drowned out, which people so desperately need to hear. What does this say to the church?

Loneliness Leads to Other Problems

Unfortunately our problem does not stop at mere loneliness. It eventuates in alienation—the feeling that one doesn't belong, that society is heartless, that everything is stacked against him. The result can be a silent and sullen resentment, a protest against the establishment, or anti-social behavior of many kinds. Public school teachers know so well that the child from a loveless home where there is tension or hostility is likely the one who is a problem in the classroom and who finds, perhaps unconsciously, a thousand ways to disrupt and rebel. It is a law of human nature that the feeling of isolation and alienation leads to hostility.

Think of how many factors and structures of society lead to this. Families are separated by staggered work schedules. Crowded and unwholesome living conditions multiply. Resentment against employers grows in an impersonal industrial complex. Artificial tastes and demands are created by modern advertising against the backdrop of affluence and glamor. For millions of people there are constant pressures which produce discontent and frustration.

Add to this the enormous injustice imposed upon minority groups, people caught in the rapid change of industry to automation amid mushrooming technology, people who have no way to prepare quickly for new forms of employment, or those caught in massive movements of the population to the already crowded areas of great urban centers. Here you see some of the powerful forces at work today that rob a man of his personhood, his sense of personal dignity and worth. The depersonalizing forces today are many and strong. They often are beyond our understanding and control. All this leads to almost overwhelming feelings of alienation from the privileged and secure minority. It's the kind of world we live in now. And we do have to live *now*.

Of course, alienation is not confined to the poor or to minority groups. It is found also among the affluent, the privileged, the educated, and the wealthy. Any professional man could point out examples of husbands and wives living under the same roof but really living in different worlds, of parents and children alienated from one another. Here is fertile soil for unrest, rebellion, and violence. People go to their doctors who spend much time treating psychosomatic patients, or to their lawyers to seek divorce, or to their ministers to achieve some solution by spiritual counsel. Psychiatrists' offices are full of people who are alienated from one another and from God.

Life is so made that a person cannot realize himself or satisfy the desires of his own heart unless he comes to terms with God, with himself, and with others. People hate because of the feeling of hopelessness and frustration, or out of their own inner distortions and conflicts. When a basic honesty —possible only as we accept God's love — leads to confession and acceptance of oneself, then the basic trend in human nature toward love and acceptance of others can be seen and relatedness can be established or restored. Here is where the fellowship of Christian love holds a key.

Loneliness or alienation lies deep. It cannot be faced and cured in a moment or by something happening from the outside. It has to be faced in solitude and in encounter between a man and God. To take refuge—or distraction—in more pleasure, greater thrills, louder noises, stronger stimulants, and temporary escapes only increases the problem. And that is just what vast numbers are doing. Such escapes may provide temporary relief, but actually they prevent the real answer from coming through. It would be a good thing if every person would compel himself periodically to be absolutely alone for an interview with himself.

Alienation is thus three-pronged: The sense of separation from a righteous God; frustration and confusion within oneself; hostility against other people and the cruel, impersonal forces found in society. All of this adds up to defeat. There is a sense of unreality, of falseness, of pretense. There is fear of being known by others. There is even subtle fear of knowing oneself. There certainly is fear of standing in the presence of God. One is out of his true "stride" or "style" of living. He must force himself to keep up appearances. He plays a role, he wears a mask, he takes refuge in things and pleasures.

All of this fails to satisfy or bring any sense of reality. So, many men who do not understand their real need for relatedness go through life accepting, and trying to live by, the substitutes. The pitiable souls who desperately try to lose themselves in drink, promiscuity, drugs, and sensuality, are really like children lost and fearful in a world that has relentlessly driven them down dead-end streets where they end up desperate and alone.

It is unfortunate, to say the least, that Christians have often condemned the symptoms rather than discerning the real sickness or offering from the rich heritage of the gospel the only real cure. You can catalogue all the sins and condemn them one by one. You can denounce the world and cry, "What's the world coming to?" But look deeper and you can see that loneliness is a sickness that has reached epidemic proportions and is being fostered further all the time by the impersonal society in which we live.

The many analyses of sociological trends, while very informative and helpful for our understanding, leave the individual just as alienated and lost as ever. It is *people* we are dealing with. When people are sick they *hurt*. And not all suffering is in the body. Perhaps the greatest anguish is that of the mind and emotions, and these are often passed on to the body.

The Sin Condition

Really, we are talking about sin, not just the sins—specific acts — but the sin *condition*. Often the underlying condition leads to and stimulates the specific acts of rebellion we call sins. Sin is self-centeredness, that is to make oneself the center of everything and live in self-reference. It is self-will, the motivation to get what you want whatever the cost to other people. Sin is idolatry—worshiping the wrong thing, turning away from the Creator to created things, serving that which was intended to be our servants. Sin is, as one theologian put it, "man's godalmightiness." This refers to his attempt to play god, his lust for power, his greed for pleasure or money or any secondary thing. It is turning from the God of love to worship self or idols created by the self. The result is a certain blindness and distortion of life's values.

In the New Testament the term sin is translated from a word in the original language which meant "to miss the mark." So it is that man misses the whole point in living, turning his back on the Creator and thus twisting his own God-given capacities and qualities into a self-defeating "house divided against itself." Alienation is the result. Where there is sin, there is a feeling of guilt. Where there is guilt, there is hostility, and such hostility is projected in all relationships.

God Calls

God called to Adam (representative man) and Eve who had violated their relationship to the Creator. They "hid themselves from the presence of the Lord." And "the Lord God called unto Adam, and said unto him, Where art thou?" Adam answered, "I was afraid, because I was naked." (See Gen. 3:8-13.) Can't you just hear that today? "I felt so naked." But God called him out into the open. He is always doing that—calling people out of their hiding places into the openness of honesty and confession.

Adam, of course, blamed Eve and she, in turn, blamed the serpent. Aren't people always blaming each other, or conditions? Sure, other people and surrounding conditions have an influence upon us, but we all know that the responsibility comes back upon us to muster up the courage and come out of our hiding places. In a genuine loving fellowship that becomes possible. We are called out of hiding into genuine community.

A lovely woman about sixty years of age was in a conference I conducted along this line of thought. She said, "I don't really know who I am. I've been pretending so long, trying so hard to please people that I feel false and unreal all the way through." She had been a professing Christian for many years. Was she really a Christian? She had lived a very acceptable life, conforming to all the standards of the church, and yet she felt isolated and alone. What was wrong? She had tried hard but she had never found real freedom. Was the church for her a community of Christian love?

A young man came to a camp. He sneered at Christians. "They're a bunch of phonies," he insisted. He had been brought up in the church. He didn't point to any gross acts of sin in any of the people, but he felt they were pretending. The church he belonged to was given to legalism with strict standards regarding dress, places of amusement, and other life patterns. But he felt that minor things were emphasized while other more important things were omitted. What happened? Where has the church failed? What can we do to be a more vital church, to be the community of Christian love? It's a responsibility laid upon all of us.

Talk Back

1. How many truly lonely people do you know? How common is this feeling?

2. What is the relation between loneliness and sin; between alienation and sin?

3. To what extent does the feeling of isolation lead to specific sins? Think of some examples.

4. At the New York World's Fair great technological achievements were displayed, but only blocks away there were slum crimes and vast human need in Harlem. Where is the problem? Why the contrast?

5. Why aren't "revivals" working the same as they once did? How can the church win people in the modern city?

6. One author (*A Drink at Joel's Place*) says a person is sometimes more likely to find acceptance and fellowship at "Joe's Place" (the bar) than at the church. What do you think of that?

Study Activity One

Let each member of the group interview at least one person he considers to be alienated or lonely, to ask about him, find out how he feels. Then report at the next session. (Use no names, of course.)

Study Activity Two

Delegate one or more of your group to talk with a campus rebel or a "far out" young person or perhaps several of them. Then have them share with the class. Better yet, invite such a young person to meet with your class for conversation. (Fasten your seat belts!)

Chapter 2

Where Does a Person Find Himself?

The age-old story Jesus told about the prodigal son (Luke 15:11-30) has in it a kind of key: "And when he came to himself. . . ." Precisely there was the turning point in his conduct. The motto on an office wall declared, "When a man comes to himself he is at home with God." Jesus said, "The kingdom of God is within you." What did he mean?

Apparently if a person really comes to terms with his own deepest nature, he will find a reality in being, a kind of true personhood. If he can sense the image in which he was created, the true nature of his being, he will be set free inwardly to realize the full development of his potential. As the seed has within it the kind of tree, the color of the blossom, the shape of the leaf, the kind and color of the fruit—even its aroma and flavor—so a person has within him the uniqueness of his own personality and vocation. Christ calls us into being! But where? And how?

It is the layers of pretense and fear, the withdrawal within oneself and from others which keeps a person from becoming genuinely himself. Counselors and psychiatrists have the difficult task of helping a person to understand what these layers are and to fold them back one by one. Many such layers could be folded back if, in a loving fellowship and friendship with other persons, one could become aware of them, and emerge with honesty and candor without fear of being rejected. But such an atmosphere of freedom is uncommon. (Perhaps one reason why people use alcoholic beverages is that they temporarily feel more "free.")

The Loving Fellowship

The fellowship of Christian people should be loving enough and honest enough to allow the real person to emerge. But too often the effect has been to squelch and repress, for in our effort to hold up a high moral standard we often have been judgmental rather than loving. So, many a lonely, guilty soul has been driven further into his fear and guilt. This, of course, is not to say the standard should be lowered or wrong condoned but that genuine Christian fellowship should convey God's forgiveness and draw out the finest in a person. Didn't Jesus do that?

If a person is to be "saved" through Christ it will be in the honesty and courage to confront himself and his real condition. He needs help to find his own real and authentic personhood. What does this mean? If Christians are to be of any help, what are they aiming at? What is it that Christian fellowship should foster in the individual?

First, in a loving fellowship one can face up to his real condition. He need not deceive himself or blame his predicament on somebody else. He need not run from himself or escape. His sense of guilt need not be covered up or evaded. He can be brutally honest with himself and accept the responsibility for his own choices. "He that covereth his sins shall not prosper." There is a cleansing in confession and honesty which brings tremendous release. Shouldn't our fellowship be a place where a person can be honest and open?

Second, in a loving fellowship he can accept and believe in his own potential. To come to himself means to accept that, too. The long-cherished secret dreams of his heart can be brought into the open. It is not vain to do this. One's highest aspiration may be a pretty good clue to his potential. If a person has been crammed into the niche of other people's expectations, or stereotyped according to their classifications, he is less than free. Like the prisoner who was put in a cell where the ceiling was six inches too low so he could never stand up straight, he may have been denied the freedom to be himself or stand tall even in his own eyes. Real personhood calls for the individuality and freedom to be all one can be. No one is really average. Where human beings are concerned the exception *is* the rule. When a group of twelve thousand men were being inducted into the army, their shoes averaged size nine. But what if the army issued twelve thousand pairs of size nine? Whose shoes would fit? A lot of men would be limping! Perhaps something like that has happened in churches where conformity is the requirement.

Third, in a loving fellowship, a person can be realistic about his limitations. Dreams can be false, perhaps planted by some person greatly admired so that we want to be like him. How many girls have dreamed of being movie stars! How many boys want to be president! The dream must be deeper than a desire for glamour. But there is the sincere and genuine desire that may lie beneath the superficial ones. Look for that. The fellowship of Christians should be the soil in which a person can realistically assess himself—*find* himself.

Fourth, in a loving fellowship, a person should be allowed to think. Conformity to other people's standards or giving in to their ideas in order to be accepted is often a sacrifice of one's own integrity. To follow someone else's path blindly or unwillingly will leave us with a certain lostness. To worship someone else's God is a secondhand religion. Millions of people have fallen into the error of simply going along with their particular peer group. It goes without saying that this is shallow and leaves one feeling lost. The church at its best challenges us to alert thinking and personal responsibility.

Fifth, a loving fellowship encourages a meaningful personal faith. Catherine Marshall quotes a minister friend who woke up one night with a four-word sentence ringing in his mind: "God has no grandsons."[1] That's right! He has only sons. Pity the man who only worships his father's god (or someone else's). Secondhand faith is a contradiction in terms. It leaves a person stunted. He may fit into the traditions of his father and be "good"—but good for what?

Many parents have seen their children grow up in that kind of secondhand relationship to God, a faith they have simply accepted, a pattern of conduct they felt obliged to follow, living in the shadow of their parents' influence. But they have seen them rebel after a while and challenge all the old beliefs and ways. What happened? If the home situation was wholesome, it may be simply the assertion of that person's individuality and the establishing of a personal intellectual integrity—thinking things through for himself.

If the situation was not wholesome at home (or perhaps at college) such a reaction may be more violent and amount to rebellion even to the point of rejecting altogether the faith and teaching in which he had been reared. The point here is not to establish blame or give a lesson on rearing children, but to suggest that every person needs to arrive at convictions of his own if his faith is to mean anything. He needs a scale of values meaningful and valid for him if he is to establish any true morality. Conformity is not necessarily righteousness. A faith that comes at the cost of intellectual integrity is hardly valid. And a faith that one accepts with no thought of his own is not a vibrant and living thing. It is more like a childhood toy he has kept for its sentimental value. Does the church, then, encourage dynamic, living faith? Or does it demand acquiesence?

Sixth, a loving fellowship will foster a sense of personal vocation. Many men have been unhappy following in their father's profession or business, when it was really not what they wanted to do or were best fitted to do. Some men are ministers simply because they were expected by parents, teachers, or pastors to go into that work.

One man followed such expectations and went to school, completing college and seminary work at considerable sacrifice, only to enter his first pastorate deeply frustrated and unhappy. He was a dedicated Christian as evidenced by his self-discipline and hard work, but he never had the feel for this work. It was not really his authentic choice. It was, therefore, an act of integrity when he gave up the pastorate and studied to be an automobile mechanic. That is what he had always wanted to do. He loved the sound of an engine more than the sound of his own voice. Here was an instance where one person had to find a freedom from even religious expectations. Does the church foster that kind of authentic personal choice?

Seventh, a genuine Christian fellowship should nurture a sense of inner freedom. One must dare to be himself. He can't go on pretending or wearing a mask or playing the role expected of him. He has to become a genuine person, unique in the true sense, a person in his own right. This means to be able to speak honestly, act frankly, think positively, and be genuinely human. In a sense it is false to do anything else. This does not infer that a person who has not found such freedom is deliberately false or hypocritical, but rather that all of us struggle with the problem at one stage or another. We know what it is to feel "phony," sometimes in a vague and ill defined way.

In Christian camps and quest groups one of the common confessions is of such a feeling of superficiality and of forced righteousness. People who are the products of fine Christian homes have said this often. Perhaps there is simply the built-in hazard of falling into a pattern of acceptance without question and of conformity without real decision. But if, in the Christian community, one is to "come to himself" it has to be in terms deeper than simply going along with the group. Shouldn't Christian fellowship encourage this kind of genuine inner freedom?

Eighth, authentic Christian fellowship will prove that personal freedom is not found in isolation from others but in relation to others. It is found in a community or group loving enough and honest enough to allow the individual to be truly himself. One needs acceptance by at least a few significant persons. Individuality has to find expression somehow in the framework of mutuality. Those who have been fortunate enough to be born into families and homes where there was genuine acceptance and love can be incredibly grateful. What a blessing that is! And those who have found a Christian fellowship where there was genuine Christian love rather than judgmental attitudes which demanded conformity can also be grateful.

More Than a Number

With these characteristics of what makes a person real in mind let us turn to some of the influences and forces which rob us and depersonalize us. We live in a climate of protest against such influences. One underlying motif in all such protest is the mute cry, "Look, I'm a person—not a number, not a place on the assembly line, not another degree being ground out by the educational machine, not merely a member of a race or group. I'm an individual with feelings, hopes, and dreams." Can you hear that cry?

The protest is against everything—or nearly everything —that is part of the establishment. It is a protest against big business, big government, big church, or big university. It objects to making man just a part of the crowd. It is restless amid the homogenizing of society where our thinking is handed out by the opinion-makers, and the desire-creators who would mold and shape human beings into something like little zombies, automatons, or moral pygmies.

There is a tremendous and widespread reaction to the whole standardizing process that cuts out everybody according to the same pattern. My mother used to cut out cookies from a rolled out piece of dough, while I stood with my chin hooked over the edge of the table, drooling in anticipation. Her cookie cutter had a bent place on one side, and—wouldn't you just know it—every cookie had a crooked side! Cookies don't rebel, but people do!

The irony of it is that usually the only way a person can protest successfully is en masse. If you speak alone no one hears you. If a laboring man speaks alone to the massive industrial machine, he is ignored or fired. So we have massive labor movements and the laboring man becomes a part of two massive machines instead of just one. If a student speaks alone against the vast educational structure, he is ignored or flunked. So we have mass student movements of protest. But the student becomes a cog in another mass movement and now is caught between them. Ironically enough, the movements of protest are often more depersonalizing than what they protest. Behold, how they dress alike and use the same language of protest.

So it is that in our modern society mass moves against

mass, bloc against bloc, ethnic group against ethnic group, race against race, and right against left. It happens on an international scale as one "ism" confronts another and little countries are overrun again and again by the horror called war. It is true even in religion where the "isms" challenge the "wasms" and people are almost forgotten. The channels of information and news are so dominated and controlled by vested interests, ideological biases, and ulterior purposes that the little man who wishes to think for himself is given really very little reliable and impartial information to provide grist for his intellectual mill.

What Can We Do?

It is in this dynamic tension that we minister. Where can we take hold? How can we sift out the real issues and think for ourselves? Even religious leaders are apt to fall into a classification and become a part of some massive movement where a few people dominate the thinking, do the speaking and the writing, meet the press, and get their faces on television. While such movements may start with the finest of aims they—even they—can quickly become corrupted by power and infiltrated by those who have their own ulterior designs. How can we relate to all this as a Christian fellowship?

How does a man come to himself in all this? What is real personhood and how can it be established in such a climate? How can we avoid a nameless, faceless, meaningless existence when apparently our only alternative to one massive machine may be another one with even less responsible leadership? And how, in any case, can we make our voices heard or make any meaningful contribution by trying to stand or act alone?

Talk to half a dozen people at work or on the street. See what organizations they belong to. Ask how they came to be members. Find out how much they really are involved in making the decisions in those organizations. See how much they know about them; how the membership money and other fees are accounted for and how well they understand reports, if any are given. Try to ascertain just how much they have turned over their thinking to other people and how much they "goose step" to somebody else's music.

Now go a step further and discuss in your group or class just how much of your Christian standard and thinking has been inherited from your parents and how much of it you have really thought through for yourselves. To what degree are you the product of a "denominational" pattern?

Talk Back

1. Have you been free to express how you really think and feel to other members of the group? Is the spirit and relationship within your class or group such that you would dare to speak frankly?

2. What would be your inner reaction if someone came up with a wild and unorthodox idea in your class?

3. Of the people you know, how many would have to be called phony? How many conformists? How many creative thinkers? How many really contribute in their organizations?

Study Activity

If your group is over twelve people break up into small groups of not more than ten or twelve (preferably smaller); then ask each one to respond to this question: To what extent do you feel you have found real personal freedom to think, to act on your real convictions, and to serve God according to your real abilities?

Then report the findings back to the total group.

---

[1]Catherine Marshall, *Beyond Our Selves* (New York: McGraw-Hill Book Co., 1961), pp. 47, 48.

Chapter 3

The Vocation of Reconciliation

Christ calls us into *being!* And into *doing.* The being comes first. First the new life in Christ, then the sharing. First, like the disciples, "to be with him," then to go out and bear witness to his power. Worship and work, inbreathing and outbreathing, "inward journey" and "outward journey" (as coined by Elizabeth O'Conner)—this is the rhythm. Our religion is placed in an artificial and false position if it is confined behind the doors of an ecclesiastical enclosure or expressed only through a kind of impersonal broadcasting medium.

Both the content and the communication of our message will change radically for the better when it issues once again through the voices and actions of people in the halls of education, in the laboratory of scientists, in the marketplace of trade, in the factories and shops where countless significant Christians spend most of their waking hours. Too long the message has been heard only from the "clerics in their unanswerable pulpits." It needs to be mediated and expressed—in being and doing—through the life's work and the language known where people toil and struggle.

Everyone Is Called

The men who gathered around Jesus were ordinary men—laymen, if you please. There were fishermen, a tax collector, a political revolutionary (zealot), and others. Not one of them was a religious "pro." Jesus himself was not of the priestly tribe of Aaron. He was not a Levite. He was a layman! He taught his followers in a close-knit and intensive fellowship, then sent them out to bear his message and to prepare the way for his coming (Matt. 10:1-16). Fishermen, yes, but he made the sweeping promise that he would *make them* "fishers of men." You can hardly imagine a more impulsive and bungling fellow than Peter—anything but a "pro"—but he became a power, with his native abilities cleansed, disciplined, enhanced, and endued with a power beyond himself. Or, take James, fisherman brother of John. He isn't very prominent in the Gospel accounts, but his native abilities were blessed and increased so that he became a kind of balance wheel in times when differences of opinion could have been serious. (See Acts 15.)

The late Samuel Shoemaker used to say that so much religious activity is the "pros talking among themselves." He spoke of the great gap between the church and the world and the need for a good "worldly sense." Could it be that some of these ordinary laymen would have something vital to say in the church about the world, that they might have a perspective or viewpoint the church needs to make its program vital in everyday life and skills from which the church could greatly profit?

According to the New Testament, every Christian is a *called* person—called by God into being and doing. This calling (vocation) does not really have reference primarily to one's occupation or the way he makes his living, but rather to the overarching, permeating purpose of his life. But this isn't all. Each of us is invited to be a part of the *called company* of God's people. The personal calling is in the framework of the called people.

Our concern here is with the *corporate obedience* to God and how we respond to God's will as a body. Personal obedience is vital, but not enough. The pastor is distinguished among his people, not because he alone is a called person but by the peculiar function he has among them as pastor, teacher, and equipper. (See Eph. 4:11-13.) The whole church is a ministry. The pastor is to teach, encourage, guide, and support every Christian in expressing his own vocation. All Christians are called, including the pastor. The calling can and does extend to the way in which one can best obey God according to his own unique abilities.

The Church Is Called

The church is a called company of people—called out from the ways of rebellion, alienation, and sin; called into a vital relationship with God; called to active involvement with God in what he is doing in the world. Israel, in Old Testament times, was called as a people. They were united in a sense of destiny, called to carry out a mission. They were called into being as a nation (or people) to have a part in God's purpose in history. He had promised the Messiah and that was their hope.

The Ephesian letter speaks of the Christian church in the New Testament times as "called to the one hope that belongs to your call" (4:4). The Apostle Paul enjoined them to "walk worthy" of their calling and to keep the unity of the spirit in the bond of peace and harmony.

Thus, the individual is a called person in the midst of a called people. He doesn't stand alone. He is sustained, supported, guided, even corrected in the fellowship. His gifts and abilities, whatever they may be are "for the common good." That is, he contributes to the life of the body of believers as well as bringing his witness to bear outside the fellowship. Whatever he can do, then, is conserved by the fellowship, and the whole ministry of the whole people carries forward under the Holy Spirit.

Each person is a priest in the sense that he ministers to others. The whole church is a ministry through the servant-hood taught and demonstrated by Jesus (Phil. 2:5-11). It is a mistake to think and act independently. You never "walk worthy" alone. It is in fellowship, cooperation, and harmony. Of course, the calling has deep personal meanings but these are within the framework of God's own purpose and plan which includes all his people across the span of history. Personal fulfillment is realized in that relationship.

Called to Reconcile

The church must be thought of as a covenant people— under a covenant with God. His testament is a covenant with us. We are committed to him. He reached out to us in unconditional love. We respond to him in unconditional surrender. We are not our own. Like Paul, we admit that this is not something we have laid hold of but something which has laid hold of us. We are his by right of creation. We are his by right of redemption. The initiative belongs to him. "Ye have not chosen me," said our Lord, "but I have chosen you, and ordained you" (John 15:16). Having heard that call we have entered into a covenant of obedience. We accept his purpose as our purpose.

And what is his purpose? Reconciliation! Reconciling man to his God first of all. "Repent," he cried, "for the kingdom of heaven is at hand." Give up the load of guilt and know his forgiveness. Raise the white flag of personal surrender and come under his lordship, a subject of his kingdom whose law is the law of love. Be a part of his new order that has the seeds of the future in it. Forgive your fellowman and seek his forgiveness so that there need be no barriers to divide and destroy.

Give yourself up. "A house divided against itself cannot stand." Nor can a person who is inwardly divided, in whose mind and heart rage a civil war. Reconciliation must be thoroughgoing if we are to find peace. "God was in Christ reconciling the world to himself." There's the heart of it all, and our calling is to share in it, for he has "committed unto us the word of reconciliation" (2 Cor. 5:19).

This ministry of reconciliation becomes our vocation. He who came to reconcile now carries forward his work through his people, his "body." The sickness of loneliness and alienation so prevalent in the days of the first century church seems to be even greater now. That ancient society was fractured by deep cleavages between Jew and Gentile, slaves and free men, Greeks and "barbarians." It was a social structure held together largely by force of Roman soldiers. Rebellion and insurrection were in the air. Even the tiny nation of Jewish people was restless and ready for a radical leader, ready to hurl themselves against the powerful Roman forces in even a suicidal attempt to gain their freedom. Religious bigotry distorted the view of man. The walls of hostility were high and thick. Into this very climate marched the church of Christ with its incredible ministry and message of love and reconciliation. The driving motivation and the guidelines are given in the second letter to the Corinthians (5:14-21). Look at that in the New English Bible.

To Tell What God Has Done

"The love of Christ leaves us no choice," cried the inspired Apostle, "when once we have reached the conclusion that one man died for all" (v. 14). There is the basis of all our ministry—what God has done. God revealed and demonstrated his unconditional love for man, and out of that overwhelming fact comes our motive and reason for even attempting to engage in any ministry among our fellowmen.

We have nothing to offer of ourselves. We have no ministry of our own. We have no right to go about setting anybody else straight or leading them to any different life as though we are superior to them. Everything we do stems from the self-disclosure of God and the revealing of his love and will. We are but bearers of that wonderful message and instruments of that love. The only real ministry, then, is the ministry of Christ. It is the love of Christ which "constrains" us. Not that we always feel that overpowering love and are thus compelled by a motivation in spite of our will. No, the power lies in the fact that we believe in what he has done, and whether we feel like it or not we have no choice but to act on it. The motivation lies not in feeling but in faith, not in whim but in will.

"His purpose in dying for all was that men, while still in life, should cease to live for themselves, and should live for him" (v. 15). There is the turning point! And that is what Christianity means. At that point one becomes a minister of reconciliation. The self-gratifying forms of worship and church life can leave us so ingrown, so unaware of the heartache and pain of those around us, taken up with religious entertainment and subtly proud of our charitable acts and churchly activities. In the light of God's unconditional love, our only appropriate response is unconditional surrender of our way to his. To live for him is to live for his purpose, and that purpose is reconciliation.

"With us therefore worldly standards have ceased to count in our estimate of any man" (v. 1b), said the Apostle. How many people of Paul's time had been written off as of no account. They were mere "dogs" or "heathen." They didn't belong. They were "strangers," "uncircumcised," "without hope and without God" (Eph.

2:11-22, NEB). Anyone who was not a Jew was an alien. So the classifications were neat and tidy, the standard was held high to preserve national dignity and ethnic purity. But the Apostle insisted, "Now in union with Christ Jesus you [Gentiles] who once were far off have been brought near through the shedding of Christ's blood" (v. 13).

That overpowering, divine act wipes out barriers and creates a new humanity. "For he is himself our peace. Gentiles and Jews, he has made the two one, and in his own body of flesh and blood has broken down the enmity which stood like a dividing wall between them . . . so as to create out of the two a single new humanity in himself, thereby making peace. This was his purpose: to reconcile the two in a single body to God through the cross, on which he killed the enmity" (vv. 14-16). How can the worldly standards by which people are classified count for anything among Christians when Christ has provided the basis for a new order in love?

Yet in today's world—even today's church—such worldly and unjust standards have counted far too much. Whole segments of our population have been branded, marked, stereotyped, and practically written off, regardless of the intrinsic worth of persons.

Get Past the Barriers

The ministry of reconciliation simply cannot be content with these cleavages among people. It brings the dissolving power of love to bear upon barriers. It meets every person as a person and introduces the redeeming power of God. No genuine Christian can accept as normal and right the inequalities which exist in the human family.

The cleavages and fractures on the basis of race or wealth or culture are morally wrong, socially explosive, and intellectually indefensible. They just do not make sense in a time like this. The color of a man's skin has nothing whatever to do with his worth as a person or his potential abilities. Christians ought to be people with whom such worldly standards and artificial distinctions have "ceased to count." If the church simply reflects conditions around it and if, within its own ranks, it continues the same distinctions, then what?

"When anyone is united to Christ, there is a new world," says the Apostle, "the old order has gone, and a new order has already begun" (2 Cor. 5:17, NEB). His personal life is indeed changed and all things have become new, but the basis, also, for a new social order has been laid. When a person's hostility and prejudice give way to love, he starts to live out the love of God in his relationships. His influence changes. He becomes a factor toward the creation of understanding and the building of bridges for communication. "Blessed are the peacemakers: for they shall be called the children of God." What better role for the Christian and the church to fulfill! But this is no mere personal matter, nor a passive kind of influence. The vocation of reconciliation calls for active, imaginative involvement. We must *look* for ways, and *seek* the means by which we can engage in such ministry. The church as a community of Christian love becomes the base in which we experience oneness and go out to serve.

"From first to last," says the Scripture, "this has been the work of God. He has reconciled us men to himself through Christ, and he has enlisted us in this service of reconciliation" (v. 18). Note the word *service*. Our Master gave himself completely in service to people in need. He "came not to be ministered unto but to minister." No one else ever poured out his life as did Jesus.

In his last hours with the disciples before he went to the cross, he observed the traditional Passover meal which symbolized sacrifice and deliverance, then gave to them the broken bread and the wine that symbolized his own broken body and blood telling them by this what it meant to go all the way in reconciling love. Then he girded himself with a towel, poured water into a basin, and, like a common slave, washed their feet. There he set before them, and before us, the spirit of his own life and of those who would follow him truly. The "service of reconciliation" takes countless forms. It meets people at the point of their needs—physical, mental, social, or spiritual—and serves. No wonder the church was referred to as the servant people.

"God was in Christ" the Scripture continues, returning to the central theme, "reconciling the world to himself . . . he has entrusted us with the message of reconciliation" (v. 19). After the service comes the message. After the loving deed the loving word takes root. Not the deed alone nor the word alone but both in Christ's spirit. Perhaps there may be time or opportunity for only the deed or the word, but, given in his name, it will have meaning. Being the community of Christian love means both serving and witnessing.

We Are Ambassadors

"We come therefore as Christ's ambassadors . . . as if God were appealing . . . through us: in Christ's name, we implore you, be reconciled to God!" (v. 20). Do we dare believe that Christ's own ministry is exercised through us? Yes! Unworthy as we are, it is true. "We have this treasure in earthen vessels." The local congregation can become a community of Christian love, a redemptive atmosphere, a loving, healing fellowship. Out from that fellowship one goes a witness to what God has done through Christ and also what God has done among his people. A person can do that if he has experienced it in his church.

Christians are intercessors. An intercessor is one who stands between. He is one who may be called upon to endure fatigue and conflict, caught in the crossfire of misunderstanding, and humiliated by hostile reaction. Jesus was. He embraced the poverty of the manger, the lowliness of the servant, the austere simplicity of one who had no place to lay his head. But God "raised him to the heights" (Phil. 2:5-13). He is the Great Reconciler.

More than anything else, our world needs a whole army of reconcilers, waging peace, storming the entrenchments of prejudice, hostility, ignorance, poverty, and sickness. Such ministry is both an individual and a group responsibility as we live out our days in the common ventures of work and play, in neighborhood or factory or office, in church or school. We can do so having received strength ourselves in the community of Christian love. If ever the massive and deeply entrenched problems of human relations are to be successfully met, there will have to be massive and concerted action by the reconcilers. That is the finest function of the church.

Talk Back

1. A ministry of reconciliation necessarily involves individual action and action by the church as a loving fellowship. List on the board ways in which the *church* can act.

2. What would your line of work, with its necessary skills and understanding, have to say to the church about its work? How could we profit by putting some of that know-how to use in planning the program of the church?

3. How can we as a church tackle the problem of discrimination against minority groups? How can we help bridge the gaps and establish friendly relations?

Study Activity

Find some responsible and representative spokesman from a minority group, if you can, and invite him to tell the group how he and his people feel. Ask questions. Get their real viewpoint.

Chapter 4

Alive in Fellowship

A young mother had utterly lost her way. Inner turmoil became so intense that she began using intoxicating drink to relax and temporarily forget. Her early homelife had been unhappy and she had been a desperately lonely child. Craving affection, she willingly yielded herself to a young man and had conceived a child out of wedlock. The young man and she finally married, but they had little real respect for each other. Whatever temporary affection they felt was mingled with hostility.

It was a shaky relationship. They argued. They accused each other. And the little child was caught, helplessly, in tension and conflict so that he was ill. There was never real fidelity, on her part at least. There were other men who came and went. Finally her husband left her, taking the child with him.

The woman was unable to find work for she had never developed her natural abilities. In addition, she had an unpleasant disposition that allowed no one to get along with her. She was still drinking when she could find the money, and she used her body in the age-old way to earn what little she got. Then liquor seemed unable to bring any escape from herself. She started to use narcotics, just a little at first, then more and still more. She was inwardly and outwardly lost, desperate, and afraid. Everyone seemed to be against her.

Then one day a woman who knew her invited her to go

with her to a prayer group, of all places! It all seemed very strange to her but in her desperate need for some understanding she went. It was an open group with women from three different congregations who had been hungry for deeper fellowship and more meaningful worship. Knowing she would be coming, they made a covenant among themselves that they would, in Christ's name, give her not judgment but love. There would be no criticism, no condescending attitudes, no superior feelings, only love. As Christ had loved them and forgiven them in spite of their unworthiness and sin, so they would try to love and accept her as a person created in God's image. She came.

They simply prayed and shared while she stayed aloof at first in a kind of stunned and stony silence. But she came again and again. Gradually the barriers were lowered, and she began to ask an occasional question. At length she spilled out some of her deep feelings, confessed some of her desperate loneliness, even some of her sin. All was met in love. She was never rejected. They really loved her—for her own sake and in spite of her great wrong.

At last she surrendered her whole life to Christ. She was a transformed person! When I met her she was radiant and happy, negotiating and talking with her husband about reestablishing their home. It would be a long process and an uphill climb, but she was excited, hopeful, and happy.

What happened there? Did the women of that prayer group compromise their Christian standards by taking her in? Can you accept a person, as a person, even when you know he is immoral and wicked? Can you do it without looking down on him? How does Christ love us? How did he love Mary of Magdala or Zacchaeus? Do you think that in our anxiety to hold up the standard of righteousness we just might have overlooked the love of Christ and its power to heal?

Redemptive Groups

All across America and in other parts of the world as well, there has been a ground swell of small groups that have sought to recapture the genius and power of a deeper fellowship. In many larger congregations such groups have come together for study of the Bible, for prayer, for study of current issues, and such. One scholar made a compilation of reports[1] which served as an encouragement and guide for many additional ones since. Whole movements have arisen among these groups such as one composed primarily of business and professional men who constantly face complex problems where it is not always clear just what is the Christian course of action.

Such quest groups have simply transcended denominational lines as sincere Christians have felt the need for honest, face-to-face confrontation and dialogue-in-depth. It is one of the most exciting and wholesome developments in modern Christendom. Housewives gather for coffee after children have gone to school. Businessmen gather for lunch or even breakfast. Couples gather for an evening. Many of these discover a deep spiritual relatedness and meaning.

It seems more like the New Testament church than do many of the large (or small) services of worship where all the light comes in one window at the front (the pulpit) and we have no opportunity to speak out of our hearts or to hear one another. The loneliness of our time actually carries over into the church where, while we may be in a large group, we are essentially alone. There is often no real engagement of the mind and heart.

When We Meet in His Name

Jesus promised something tremendous to his disciples, and they believed it! "Where two or three are gathered together in my name, there am I in the midst of them"

(Matt. 18:20). They really believed that, even after he had gone from them in the flesh. If you read the Acts of the Apostles with awareness, you will sense that they lived and labored in the consciousness of the presence of the risen Christ. Their early form of worship was by coming together to share a common meal (a pitch-in dinner, if you please) followed perhaps by a period of instruction and discussion. Each person would contribute what he could—a psalm, a hymn, or whatever. (See Ephesians 5:19 and 1 Corinthians 14:26.) They seem to have observed very frequently the Lord's Supper or Communion, remembering their Lord as he instructed them on that never-to-be-forgotten evening before his crucifixion. In that deep awarenesss of his own presence and open to one another in loving fellowship, they knew a power that was nothing short of phenomenal. History attests to that!

Meeting "in his name" means more than lip service. It means in his spirit and purpose. (A name meant that in those days.) That is what made the church; the coming together in a unique and dynamic kind of relationship. It was the genius of their *relationship,* rather than a building, organization, or ecclesiastical heritage, that gave power. Their identity as a group was tied not to something visible or earthly but to a spiritual quality and a sense of mission in spreading that quality of life like a leaven in the dough of society. Christ was present among them, and his rule there was the central reality of it.

But to come "in his name" meant also a certain openness to one another, a self-exposure as persons, and an honesty about their needs. The Apostle James, a longtime leader in the Jerusalem church, urged them to "confess your faults [sins] one to another, and pray one for another, that ye may be healed" (James 5:16). He also insisted that they should not show partiality or extend any special recognition or favor to the wealthy and privileged (James 2:1-9). It would seem from the account in the Acts of the Apostles that rich and poor were united in one, sharing their goods and treasure, uniting in a loving fellowship (Acts 2:44-46).

Nor was there a difference made between clergy and laymen. They all made up the "whole people of God." The apostles, no doubt, had great influence because they had been with Jesus through his ministry and were witnesses to the resurrection. But "the ground was level at the foot of the cross," and they had all things in common.

Strength from Each Other and God

It is interesting to see what happens in a camp or retreat when clerical garb, titles, and distinctions are laid aside and people come to know their pastors and leaders as real and quite ordinary persons. The whole atmosphere changes when a preacher puts on a sport shirt and strikes out at softball with a high school boy doing the pitching. Why? The barriers come down and persons meet more as persons. It is even more remarkable when in a group of honest, questing people, we get sincere and frank about our problems and needs—when we take off the masks and quit playing roles; when we stop putting up a front while trying to make a good impression.

Something vital takes place when we reveal our real hungers, for always there are others there who have the same hungers. If you join two insulated wires, what happens? Nothing! If you strip away the insulation and join the wires themselves, what happens? The current flows! If people come together for worship wearing their masks and carefully insulating themselves against being known in any real way, what happens? Nothing! If they come as real persons, honest persons, confessing their needs and failures, what happens? Something dynamic and vital!

"Where two or three are gathered in my name, *there am I.*" A new dimension is added. A condition is fulfilled. A power is released.

Thus we draw strength from one another and from our Lord, and the true church comes into being. Fellowship is redemptive and healing where love flows through it. The fellowship of the New Testament was a life-sharing relationship in the life of Christ. We belong to one another because we belong to him and because we are together in him.

Is there any cure, then, for the alienated, lonely, lost person who feels no one cares for him or understands him? Yes. If the church is real there is indeed a cure. It is no "compromise" to love—even where someone has stooped to the most sinful kind of life. Christ wants to save, even to the uttermost. It is not the Father's will that any should perish but that all should come to repentance and wholeness.

New Life in Christ

The basis of community and the cure for alienation is in Christ. To know and believe in God's love is the beginning of a new life. "In this was manifested the love of God toward us, because that God sent his only begotten Son into the world, that we might live through him. Herein is love, not that we loved God, but that he loved us, and sent his Son to be the propitiation [remedy] for our sins" (1 John 4:9-10). There is no full cure on the horizontal level alone. A person needs to get right with God by genuine honesty and confession and by simple faith in God's mercy and love. But this love is mediated through the fellowship of Christian love.

The church is the custodian of the gospel, with its good news of what God has done. Its main message is not good advice but good news. Therefore, its work begins by confronting a man with that central fact. Fellowship begins with the redemptive act in the individual heart. (One could be accepted and loved by a group of people but still have guilt in his heart.) At the threshold of the fellowship and central in its very life is the *new life* in Christ.

Genuine fellowship might be called the earthly counterpart of divine love. "When the day of Pentecost had come, they were all together in one place" (Acts 2:1). There the condition was fulfilled. Hearts were united. There was a period of ten days during which time, no doubt, the selfish ambitions of James and John, the fear of people that had caused Peter to deny his Lord—these and countless other obstructions were relinquished and one by one the people had made a full surrender to God. Only then could the Holy Spirit come in his power. Even those who were spectators were powerfully affected and some three thousand were saved.

Fellowship is more than the absence of a fight. And it is more than a camaraderie, a jovial and friendly kind of relationship. Wholesome as that is, the fellowship of the spirit is deeper, more meaningful, more rewarding. When we can know one another as seeking persons, sharing our hungers and problems, then our hearts are united in one. We "bear one another's burdens" and so fulfill Christ's law of love. We discover that in the midst of seeking, honest persons there is another Person present, a power added, a new dimension realized.

Love in the Fellowship

This is indeed the cure for alienation. The lonely, self-contained, self-conscious person can let down the barriers of fear and come out of his defensive shell into the open. Alienation is melted away by love—the love of God and of his people.

It is in such genuine fellowship that this love is mediated. This is done through the quality of relatedness and through the reality of Christ's love. The church is intended to be like that. It does not come by the pseudosophisticated aloofness that leaves people still estranged from one another, nor the critical, judgmental pressure which crams everyone into a rigid mold, requiring conformity even at the expense of personal honesty.

In a genuine fellowship we draw strength from one another and from him whose Presence sustains it. We know the meaning of intercessory prayer for one another. As we become aware of the inner struggles, the real needs, we sense a deep kinship for we have the same or similar needs. We know then that we are not so unusual after all. We are all part of the same human race with about the same struggles.

But so long as we wear the masks that hide our inner needs and longings, the insulation keeps us from any living encounter with other people or with God. To love in this sense is to be aware of *reality* in others—that is the real person and his deep yearnings. To thus sense reality in other persons is to be ready to sense the reality of God. How can you say you love God whom you haven't seen if you don't love your fellowman whom you can see?

There is true reconciliation, the answer to alienation and fear. The church as a fellowship of love has vastly more than itself to offer. It has a divine as well as human dimension. "Where two or three are gathered together in my name, there am I."

But it is most unfortunate when a quest group becomes ingrown and pharisaical in its spirit. That denies its very nature and purpose. A group *can* be a most effective and powerful means of outreach. If an average congregation, especially in the large city, consecrated itself for the task and took some basic training, it could start in its own homes redemptive groups among neighbors and friends. These might become extensions of the church's fellowship and outposts of service and reconciliation.

The church at its best has employed the small group approach. Jesus himself drew his disciples together for intensive training, then sent them out. The first century church certainly employed this form of worship and training. John and Charles Wesley used it very widely.

Spiritual renewal has been attended by this principle of person-to-person encounter and spiritual power. Now we see it increasing over the land. It needs direction and encouragement, not resistance. People cannot live in a vacuum. They must live in relationships. What *kind* of relationship is the question. How will we in the church respond?

TALK BACK

1. Have you ever been in a group where there was genuine and honest sharing of needs, hungers, or problems? What is your reaction? Tell the group about your experience.

2. In what ways, if any, is your congregation reaching out in loving fellowship to those who are lonely and lost?

3. Some work has been done among people of a given occupation, either on-the-job or off-the-job environment. Do you see any possibilities for such an outreach?

Study Activity

Ask your pastor for guidance and conduct an experiment with some occupational group or some neighborhood group. See if you can establish a new pattern of outreach through the use of a small group.

---

[1]John Casteel, *Spiritual Renewal Through Personal Groups,* (New York: Association Press, 1957).

Chapter 5

The Church—Biblical Concepts

As Jesus neared the end of his earthly ministry he showed increasing concern over the future of the cause to which he had so completely given himself. From the time when he observed the traditional Passover meal with his disciples to the time when he went to the cross, he spoke much about the ministry of the Holy Spirit whom he promised to send, and about the relationship of his followers to one another and to God. The Apostle John recorded these discourses most adequately in chapters thirteen through sixteen in the Fourth Gospel.

The Church Dynamic

We do not see the true nature of the church until we see it in terms of Christ's ongoing purpose, the continuation of his work for the redemption of man. That is to say we cannot properly conceive of the church in static terms—as institution or organization merely. It must be understood in *dynamic* terms, as movement, ministry, service, redemption. It is the continuing redemptive activity of our Lord in the world. The church is called the Body of Christ. It embodies his spirit and purpose and is the instrument or agent through which he continues his ministry. We, therefore, have no ministry of our own. There is only the ministry of Christ through his people. In a sense the church is the extension of the incarnation.

Thus, the *nature* of the church and the *mission* of the church are really two sides of the same reality for its nature is mission and its mission is inherent in its nature. It is no mere organization. It is an organism—a living body, and the human body is used as an illustration of its nature and function (Romans 12). One noted theologian laid great stress upon the nature of the church as dynamic and moving rather than static and institutional and pronounced an eloquent rebuke upon much of the existing church.[1] The purpose in this chapter is to point up the characteristics of the New Testament church as it was seen by the apostles. To make as unbiased an approach as possible, let us begin with our Lord's own references during the time when his total being was so much occupied with the future of his work.

In John 15:1-11 Jesus drew the analogy of vine and branches to illustrate the relationship between himself and his followers. "I am the vine," he said; "you are the branches" (v. 5). This is an *organic* relationship. He speaks of what we might call a mystical or spiritual organism. Life flows from vine to branch—and through the branch—to bear fruit, and its fruit is fruit of the vine, not merely of the branch. "As the branch cannot bear fruit by itself, unless it abides in the vine, neither can you, unless you abide in me" (v. 4).

The relationship indicated by the preposition *in* is one far more intimate than we commonly think. To be *in* him means just that—to share in his life, to receive strength from his, to be a part of his "body"—a spiritual body, of course, but nonetheless real. This kind of spiritually-organic relationship is seen again and again in the New Testament. "If any one is *in* Christ, he is a new creation" (2 Cor. 5:17).

Such references do not indicate merely trying hard to

follow his teachings. They reveal a kind of sharing in his very life and power, bearing his "fruit" (and "much" fruit at that), being part of a living, spiritual organism. How different that is from the formality of mere church membership! Indeed the word *member* has a radically different meaning when you speak of a member of the human body as the Apostle did in Romans 12.

It should be remembered that Christ is central in all this. It is his presence and power that gives the church life and meaning. Without him there is no living vine however many branches may be gathered together. The church in the scriptural sense is not a brush pile; it is a vine, living, fruit bearing and beautiful!

The Church, Its Lord, Its Mission—Inseparable

In his promises relating to the Holy Spirit, Jesus spoke in terms of his equipping and enabling power. The Holy Spirit was to teach his people (John 14:26). He, the Spirit of truth, was to guide them into all truth (16:13). He was to testify of Christ (15:26). He was to convict and convince the "world" (16:8). He was to make them witnesses with power (Acts 1:8).

All this relates, as you see, to the ongoing mission and work of Christ. It makes only partial sense in any other context of thought. The church, its Lord, its mission and task are all one and to be separated from one is to be separated from all. A person cannot find himself as a Christian except as he finds himself in the Body. There is something about Christ's work that is incomplete until we are one in him. He fills us so that we may fulfill him.

In our Lord's prayer recorded in John 17 he was most poignantly concerned about his people, their relationship to one another and to the world as well as to himself. Note some of the characteristics of this relationship as implied there. "I am praying for them; I am not praying for the world but for those whom thou hast given me, for they are thine; . . . and I am glorified in them" (vv. 9-10). This is not to imply that Jesus was no longer concerned about the world but that he was counting on his people to carry his message and share his burden for the world. He once instructed his disciples to "pray . . . the Lord of the harvest to send out laborers into his harvest" (Matt. 9:38). He didn't instruct them to pray that the harvest would be reaped in some miraculous fashion and the sheaves come marching in. He depends upon his people to carry out the mission. If the proper conditions are met among his people the outreach in evangelism will be a natural consequence.

Then he goes on in his prayer. "And now I am no more in the world, but they are in the world, and I am coming to thee" (John 17:11). Catch the significance of that. "I am no more in the world [in the flesh]." The entire enterprise is left with them under the guidance of the Holy Spirit. What an awesome responsibility! What a high and holy honor he has given us, and what a colossal task he has entrusted to us.

No wonder he prayed, "Holy Father, keep them in thy name . . . that they may be one, even as we are one" (v. 11b). How very important it is to be kept in God's holy name, that is, his purpose and spirit. Only so long as that vital relationship is kept intact can his purpose be fulfilled. "While I was with them, I kept them in thy name . . . I have guarded them. . . . But now I am coming to thee; . . ." (vv. 12-13). What is now to keep them in his name? What safeguards are there? Only that he has given us God's Word (v. 14)!

Earlier in this period of discourses Jesus had told them, "You are already made clean by the word which I have spoken unto you" (15:3). That's the safeguard! The

Word. At the heart of the church is the Word. Jesus himself was "the word made flesh," the pure, clear witness from God. Always the Word corrects, chastises, cleanses, exhorts, reproves, and strengthens the church.

When the Word is neglected the whole cause sags and falters. When the Word is lifted up, new conviction is implanted in every heart and character is strengthened. Without strong emphasis on the Word there is no strong conviction. Where there is no strong conviction there is no motivation to win others and there is no strong church. There has been only one time in all history when the Word came through with *full* clarity and meaning. That was in Christ. The church is always in need of his correction, comfort, and empowering.

"Sanctify them in the truth; thy word is truth" (v. 17). To sanctify means to cleanse, to separate, to consecrate or hallow. It is to make inwardly whole. It does not mean sanctimonious or "holier than thou" but full devotion to the cause. How often the cause of Christ has been made to suffer and the church robbed of power because of selfish and small motives on the part of some who professed his name!

But what of the relationship of the church to the world? "As thou didst send me into the world, so I have sent them into the world" (v. 18). There you have it. *In* the world but not *of* it, yet sent *into* it! That doesn't sound like a comfortable, isolated existence behind beautiful stained-glass windows. Jesus apparently intended that his followers should be involved in life and everyday affairs. The requirement is that we be very much in the world while living by a unique and singularly Christian scale of values. He wants us to be *in* the world but not *of* it. We have too often been *of* the world so far as values are concerned but not *in* it, in the sense of any vibrant presence or awareness.

The Church Is One

The crux, perhaps, of this prayer is Jesus' cry for unity among his followers. "I do not pray for these only, but also for those who believe in me through their word." Notice that he prays even for us today. "That they may all be one; even as thou, Father, art in me, and I in thee, that they also may be in us, so that the world may believe that thou hast sent me" (vv. 20-21).

Two points stand out there. First, the oneness (unity) is to be of the same basic kind as existed between Christ and the Father (though, I am sure, not to the same degree). It was to be *in* our Lord and the Father. Second, Jesus manifestly infers that whether the world is to believe on him as sent by God depends upon the unity of his followers. Can you think of anything more convincing to non-Christians than the demonstration of genuine unity among Christians? "By this all men will know that you are my disciples, if you have love for one another" (John 13:35). See how much hinges upon unity?

Division deals a terrible blow to any local church, robs it of its witness, makes it the laughingstock of the community. Jesus returned to the same concern near the end of that prayer. "The glory which thou hast given me I have given to them, that they may be one even as we are one, I in them and thou in me, that they may become perfectly one, so that the world may know that thou hast sent me and hast loved them even as thou hast loved me" (vv. 22-23). Glory? Yes, the glory of God and the unity of his people belong together. Unity is the glory of the Father and of the church.

It is God's purpose to unite alienated people in one fellowship of love. That is the glory and the great achievement. It is the witness of God's power in the world. Read Ephesians 2 in order to see the wonderful sweep of God's power. It begins, "And you he made alive, when you were dead" and ends, "you also are built into it [the holy temple of the church] for a dwelling place of God in the Spirit." From bondage to freedom. From captivity to creativity. From division and strife to unity. Glory to God in the church!

This was a reality, too, among those early Christians, "Now the company of those who believed were of one heart and soul" (Acts 4:32). They had a devoted fellowship together, sharing even their food (Acts 2:32). Jews and Gentiles, formerly at sharp variance, became one so Paul could say, "There is neither Jew nor Greek, there is neither slave nor free, there is neither male nor female; for you are all one in Christ Jesus" (Gal. 3:28). One spirit prevailed in their hearts; indeed "all were made to drink of one Spirit" (1 Cor. 12:13). The New Testament is replete with such references.

Key Concepts About the Church

Certain key concepts regarding the church stand out in the New Testament. One is of the *whole people of God.* The church was one fellowship without hierarchical structures. There was no bold line drawn between what we know as clergy and laity. The church was thought of as one body and God's spirit moved through all his people. The apostles themselves, while occupying, no doubt, a place of great influence because they had been with Jesus during his ministry on earth and had witnessed the resurrection, were, first of all, simply part of the whole fellowship.

The church of that time was based on an inspired membership, ministry, and government. It wasn't until years later that churchly organization which set some leaders over others was adopted and the heirarchy or power structure was developed. "There is one body and one Spirit," wrote Paul, "just as you were called in the one hope that belongs to your call, one Lord, one faith, one baptism, one God and Father of us all, who is above all and through all and in all" (Eph. 4:4-6).

Another concept is that of the *called people*. (See Chapter 3.) They were the people of God on mission. They were under covenant and contract with God.

The same holds true of the concept of *servanthood* and *ministry*. Everyone was a minister, that is, a servant. Now the word *minister* has come to mean the pastor (or clergyman). But look what has happened! Instead of the people being obedient to God's call in life, it has been made the responsibility of the minister (clergyman) to serve the church. No wonder the church is robbed of power. When we recover the concept of ministry as taught by the New Testament the church will rise in new power. So long as the burden is carried by only a few, we will be guilty of a basic heresy.

Still another basic concept which prevailed in the early church was that of *gifting by the Holy Spirit*. Everyone was to seek the divine will for his life and God set the members every one of them in the body, as it pleased him (1 Cor. 12:18). They were urged to covet the gifts of the Spirit. They depended upon the enabling power of the Spirit. In Ephesians 4, 1 Corinthians 12, and Romans 12, we have partial lists of the gifts of the Spirit. Especially in Ephesians 4 we see that there are some special gifts given in order to help, equip, and strengthen all the others. But they are not the only gifts.

We call attention to these characteristics of the church in the New Testament period, not with any thought of returning to that culture or attempting to return to its *forms* of life. What we seek is to recapture the dynamic of its spirit and its sense of mission. We seek again the primary relationships with the Living Christ and with one another. It was when the church was small and radically different in spirit from the common life of its time that it shook the world. It was in the world but not of the world, yet sent into the world.

TALK BACK

1. Take a poll among members of your group to see how they came in contact with the church. What attracted them to it?

2. How many people (what percentage) of your congregation are actively engaged in service in the church? How many are so engaged outside the church, in the community?

3. Examine the activities of your congregation. What percentage of it is planned for your own enjoyment or benefit?

4. Can your congregation be called evangelistic? What are the *means* used in evangelism?

Study Activity

Initiate, under your pastor's guidance, a study of the distribution of energy and time in your congregation. How much of it is spent primarily for the comfort and enjoyment of the members, and how much in reaching people through service and witness?

---

[1]Emil Bruner, *The Misunderstood Church,* (Philadelphia: The Westminister Press, 1953).

Chapter 6

The Church — Present Outlook

$\mathbb{W}$hat do you think of when the word *church* is mentioned? A building? A time on Sunday morning? A denomination? What image is conjured up in your mind? Now, by way of contrast, how does that image compare with the church as it is portrayed in the New Testament? Of course we must be careful not to compare mere *forms* of church life. Our point is not to decry the different forms it may have today.

In fact our point is the opposite. It is to compare essential qualities and to insist that the church should be dynamic and viable enough to adapt itself to changing needs and conditions, and to discard, when they are no longer useful, the old "established" forms. The searching question is: how many forms and structures are we holding to that are really in our way, hindering real obedience to our Lord? How many things are we doing and have forgotten *why* we do them? How much excess baggage are we carrying?

Members Inspired

The church of the first century had an *inspired membership*. Those early Christians were members of the church as branches are members of the vine or as your fingers are members of your body. They were members because they had been born of the Spirit, for "The Lord added to their number day by day those who were being saved" (Acts 2:47). They were not troubled by people who joined the church for social prestige. The persecution weeded out any of the insincere and "none of the rest dared join them, but the people held them in high honor" (Acts 5:13).

In contrast, see how church membership today is nearly meaningless so far as any real requirements are concerned. There are on church membership rolls countless thousands of names which are only that — names. There is for many no meaningful Christian commitment, no involvement in the ministry or service of the church, no exemplary Christian character or influence. When you talk to the non-Christian about becoming Christian, you often hear reactions to the effect that he is just as good as the church members. Evangelism in the scriptural sense means little in that kind of situation. Quite different from that day when, after fearless preaching of the gospel, people would cry, "What must we do to be saved?" Are we so sophisticated that we no longer need take the gospel seriously?

Leaders Inspired

The church of the New Testament had an *inspired leadership*. One didn't enter this work as a profession among other professions. He entered because he was moved to do so by a great faith and a great cause. Again and again Paul speaks of himself as called by God, unworthy as he was. The "gifts of the Spirit" were recognized and respected. They were charismatic leaders—that is, their leadership arose out of the gifts of grace. (That word *charismatic* may be given a popular and inaccurate meaning today by news media but it is, nonetheless, a valid and valuable one.) There was a divine element and quality about their work, a power which permeated the strongholds of evil and changed lives in a radical fashion.

Choosing the ministry as a profession and taking a place of status in an ecclesiastical organization is quite a different matter from the overwhelming call of God upon a person's heart. If the church is nothing more than another human organization and if it seeks leaders who will become slaves of the religious machine, always walking the treadmill of other peoples' expectations, we can expect a continuing—and increasing—exodus from its ranks. If it is simply another work of social service, then red-blooded men of imagination will often pass it by, since they might be more free for creative work outside the strictures and structures of the organized church. It is interesting to note that those groups which believe in a divinely-called, prophetic ministry are the least troubled by a shortage of ministers. Where there is no radical gospel there is no call to a prophetic, courageous leadership.

Focus on Spreading the Gospel

For about three hundred years the early Christians had few, if any, buildings. They owned no property, apparently, but met wherever they could—in homes much of the time—wherever even "two or three" were gathered in Christ's name. There were more or less established congregations and they carried on a work of ministry and witness but they were not much encumbered by material involvements. They were free to give first attention to spreading the gospel. No wonder the church grew so rapidly, even in the face of severe persecution.

But then it became entrenched, began to tie itself more and more to certain buildings, places, and programs. Its life became defined in those terms. Its identity changed from that of a powerful spiritual force to a safe and accepted part of the social structure. Such has been true, of course, ever since. The Roman Catholic church is one of the largest property holders in the world, and many

Protestant churches own vast amounts of property. Perhaps this is necessary to some degree but what has it done to our mentality, our relation to society?

It is said that a visitor was seeing for his first time a great cathedral. His guide pointed out some of its priceless art and its fabulous treasures, then remarked, "No longer can the church say, 'Silver and gold have I none.'" And the visitor pungently observed, "Neither can it say, 'Rise up and walk.'"

Flexible and Responsive

In the early days, the church was flexible, responsive to human need, alert to opportunity for witness. As we are more engrossed with our rigid structures, however, we are less aware of persons and we have less time for ministry to them. It takes a large part of our time to keep the religious machinery going. Pastors are simply loaded down with trying to keep everybody happy. The church has been so eager to get members and money, prestige and position, that it has an excessive amount of dead weight. Many of its members it would be better off without. Many local congregations are so dominated by a power structure of influential people concerned with their own position that they are almost incapable of response to the real needs around them.

It is our preoccupation with buildings, organizations, institutions, prestige, position, that robs us of ministry to people. "Let's Stop Building Cathedrals"[1] cried one noted leader in an article which deplored the insensitivity of many churches in building for the status and comfort of the privileged few rather than to carry on any real ministry. Many edifices now stand in judgment upon the pride and blindness of their builders. They are like spiritual mausoleums. In a day of depersonalizing forces in society when the human being is lonely and desperate for some real human relatedness and fellowship, that is not a very inviting picture.

The Divided Situation

Nor is the divided condition of Protestantism inviting. We have today so many divisions that the non-Christian is puzzled and repulsed. How can we speak so freely of Christian love when we are so divided? Of course denominations are the products of many influences and often reflect, not the inability of Christians to get along together, but rather the fact that they are caught up in the existing organizations and systems. Some of these divisions had their origin in historical and geographical factors, or differences in language and culture. Some denominations had their beginnings in Europe, having arisen in different countries during the Reformation.

The Reformation was, of course, a revolution against the highly organized ecclesiastical control and the corruption that so often goes along with the concentration of power. But the several denominations have tended to fall into the same kind of self-perpetuating power structures. This has led, in turn, to more revolt, and smaller denominations have been the result. Where does the problem lie? Do people start more denominations just to be divisive? Or do they want "little kingdoms" of their own? Perhaps some do, but if we look carefully we can see that often the yeast of new life could not be contained within the old rigid structures.

Sometimes prophetic voices have been silenced and "revolutionaries" expelled. Thus, a reformation is started by the revolutionaries. Then the reformation spirit which led to a new dynamic group is gradually lost and they level out into the general landscape. So, you have another denomination. Perhaps we ought to take a hard look at the rigidities which lead to revolt and reformation.

One message which seems to come through all this conflict and revolution is that we need to take our church organizations and programs less seriously and Jesus Christ more seriously! This would mean that we follow our Lord in: his concern for persons; his labor of love; his frank, plain teaching; his unconditional love; his list of priorities which, for instance, made him count man more important than the Sabbath; his defiance of the self-righteous bigot; and his loving mercy to the poor sinner.

It might even mean following him as he upset the tables of money changers and merchants of the temple and effected a kind of house cleaning. It may mean that we tangle, as he did, with the entrenched civil and religious authorities and champion the cause of justice on behalf of those who are caught in economic and moral traps. It might even mean that we pay less attention to our own financial security and follow him who had no place to lay his head. Jesus was pretty revolutionary!

So were the apostles who were accused of turning the world upside down. Sometimes the status quo must be upset in order for things to be set up justly and equitably. Demetrius, the silversmith in Ephesus, who was the chief instigator of the agitation against Paul on the ground that his preaching undercut the sale of miniature silver models of their goddess, has plenty of counterparts today. The vast industries which turn out products for the exploitation of people—the brewing industry, the tobacco industry, the narcotics rackets will not be defeated easily.

Outdated Ways

Another thing is that many of our methods and approaches and emphases are good—for the previous century! We in the church tend to lag behind. Don't we have to preserve the values and time-honored truths? Yes! But do we distinguish between what is old and established and that which is central and basic? Many church people still think in the same terms they learned perhaps in a rural or small town community and church of their youth. We follow pretty much the traditional parish pattern which prevailed when the church was the center of community life. The methods and means used in the days of a generation or more ago may feel comfortably familiar to some who are older, but most people of today have grown up in a very different kind of atmosphere. People now think in a different frame of reference.

There are powerful new social forces at work which mold life and often rob people of individuality. Clamorous voices say that just defending the status quo is, in itself, a crime against the deprived, for the status quo can be wrong—deeply, even criminally wrong. The point here is how responsive is the church? It may be that some of the voices we hear are extreme, and the very extremity seems to prove an unreliability and irresponsibility on their part. But let us ask ourselves as honestly as we know how, just how aware and responsive are we?

Get More People Involved

Another criticism levelled at the church is that a minority of its people comprise the real decision-making body, on both the local level and at "headquarters." The majority of people are onlookers, uninvolved and therefore unconcerned. Perhaps no more than 10 percent of the members of Protestant churches are actively involved in the work of the church itself, much less rendering any significant service outside.

There is widespread discontent among many who are really interested in the church and who love the cause for which it exists but who feel that fresh breezes need to be felt and new voices heard. How long can vigorous young people, whose lives are before them, be expected to go along being faithful to the church if they see no vital challenge in it? How many promising leaders have been squeezed out by persisting in "business as usual"? These are some of the alienations within the church now, the differences of viewpoint and concern.

A less articulated concern seems now to be growing over vast amounts of money tied up in buildings and grounds used for only a limited amount of time. Elaborate sanctuaries may be used for only one service of worship in the week. Well-equipped educational plants may be used a little more but not much, and there may be several such church plants within the area of a block or two. Why is so much invested in buildings when the need for ministry to people on the streets and in their homes is so great?

Why, we are asked, couldn't more than one Christian group use the same facilities at different times? Do they need the distinctive building in order to maintain some sort of identity in the eyes of the community—or even in their own eyes? Is the sense of mission not adequate to bring cohesion and loyalty? Must the church have something visible to identify itself? Can a group of Christian people carry on a meaningful program of service anyway? In the large city where property is scarce and costs are outrageous, could a Christian group use already-existing facilities—such as a downtown hotel or a school building—without serious handicap? A study of the average man in the great city reveals that the fine church edifice might actually be a hindrance in reaching people![2]

Besides this there are camp facilities across the nation where hundreds of thousands of dollars are involved. These camps are used perhaps a week during the year. And what of the hundreds of hours spent in keeping up the facilities, shaping the program, administration, and finance, only to end up with just a few leaders being able to participate in the actual purpose for which it presumably exists? Are we losing ourselves in the means to the end? Have we forgotten what the end is? Certain means, of course, are necessary, but what is our focus and emphasis? What are our measurements of success?

The central question before us is, how are we responding to present-day life and needs? The early church was open, viable, aware of people and concerned with people. In this century the church's focus of attention has concentrated on status, position, wealth, human influence, and worldly power. We have paid a heavy price for this. Often the church is passed by as irrelevant and unconcerned. But there are stirrings of a new day in the air. A revolution may be taking place in the church. Is God at work in such a revolution?

TALK BACK

1. How do you define *success*? How do you evaluate our means of achieving it? Evaluate your local church program, its facilities and methods.

2. Evaluate your area or state program of outreach for Christ. Is it effective? Why, or why not?

3. If we were starting all over to win people—if we had no property or program—how do you think we could do it best? What means and methods would we choose? The same as we have?

4. How many activities do you have in your church which you are carrying on with no real awareness of *why* you do them?

Study Activity

Delegate a small committee to make a rough estimate of the value of the church properties in your community, and figure how many hours of the week they are used. What is your impression?

---

[1]Clyde Reid, "Let's Stop Building Cathedrals," *The Christian Century,* (June 17, 1964).

[2]G. Paul Musselman, *The Church on the Urban Frontier,* (New York: Seabury Press, 1960).

Chapter 7

The Sources of Renewal

In a small city council (fictional, no doubt) the city fathers made three decisions in one day. First, they voted to build a new jail; second, to build it largely from materials in the old jail; third, to use the old jail until the new one was finished! Now, how would you do that? While carefully avoiding equating the church with a jail (though some revolutionaries would even go that far), don't we have a kind of perpetual problem like that? We have to use what we have while we find ways to build.

The challenge takes on a different meaning, however, and much more promise, when we use a solid biblical analogy—the human body—to illustrate our point. The human body is constantly renewing itself, building new cells, throwing off waste and taking in fresh nourishment. There are millions of cells in the body and these seem to be impelled to do the right thing at the right time in the right place in the right way. So it is that life pushes forward—building, repairing, casting off, feeding, and growing. So, perhaps you don't have exactly the same body you did ten years ago! That is the difference between inanimate things and living, growing, changing organisms.

Can the Church Be Renewed?

The question is whether a congregation is *inherently* capable of renewal and change. The human body can die! So can a plant or any organism. Or it can die in parts. When a limb dies on your shade tree, you cut it off for the good of the tree. Jesus said that if a branch dies on the vine, it is cut off (John 15:1)! But in the church if a branch still looks pretty much like a branch—even though there is no foliage or flower or fruit—we tend to excuse it. How many church members are that in name only? How much dead timber holds the church back from its real nature and work?

Renewal must be a constant process. The church is always in need of renewal, in every generation, in every community and every congregation. A certain amount of tension is normal: between what is and what ought to be, between the old and the new, between that which is time-honored and traditional and that which is new and demanding. Christianity is virile and dynamic when its continuity with the past and the dynamic of growth and change are kept in creative tension. It has never completely broken the thread of essentials that run from Jesus' day (and before) until now.

This continuity in itself would not be enough though. For there have been nonessentials which became millstones around the neck of the church. These had to be thrown off and new, more appropriate, essential elements taken on. Christianity is kept alive and virile by the presence of both continuity and change.[1] If we can learn that secret, it will be a notable achievement.

For renewal does not come without constant and diligent effort. It's like the boy who always wanted to be a sailor and enlisted in the Navy the very day he reached eighteen years of age. His first letter home, however, contained a note of sadness. "Dear Mom, I joined the Navy because I loved the way ships were kept so spic and span—but I never knew until this week who keeps them so spic and span."[2] Let us look at some of the resources of renewal.

Requirements for Renewal

First, we need to redefine "success." Just what is the church to be and do? When we think of a successful church what do we have in mind? A large membership? An impressive building? A popular pastor? A busy program? A large budget?

But the outward trappings of success do not necessarily go with great spiritual power. Some very small, isolated—even persecuted—church groups have been full of spiritual power. This was true in the earliest days of the church and it has been true at various times and places throughout the church's history. With or without buildings and political and economic influence, the church has been at its most significant when it has had a contagious quality of witness, when it has had people concerned with the problems of the day, when it has been able to call people into a transforming and meaningful sacred fellowship.

Success can more accurately be measured (if it has to be measured at all) in terms of ministry to people, changed lives and homes, depth of faith and dedication, and the meanings which come alive within. We need to redefine success in terms that are genuinely Christian. Where did our Lord place the premium? Would he have been considered successful by our standards of measurement?

Second, if the church is to be renewed, the responsible preaching of the Word of God must be central in its life. The tendency to discount the value and importance of biblical teaching weakens the church and its witness. Wallace Fisher properly insists,

> Forthright biblical preaching which avoids the marginal (shallow moralism) and penetrates to the heart of man's profound dilemma (guilt and meaninglessness) and speaks to his loneliness persuades persons to repent, encourages them to trust God, and

gives them identity. Linked with evangelical teaching, it motivates and equips them to exercise Christ's ministry in the world.[3]

This relates to how we view success and the role of the church in society. If the church is to be, in reality, the church, it becomes necessary, at some point, to disentangle itself from dependence on the secular support and favor it has often sought and dare to take a kind of prophetic stance. What it is to be and do will become clearer to us when we take God and his Word more seriously. The church was set in the world by God's mighty act in Christ. It is the custodian of a revelation and the channel of a power which alone can save. Thus, the gospel always judges, corrects, guides, instructs the church.

If any genuine renewal is to come, though, more than a superficial glance or occasional reference to the Word is called for. Robert Raines quotes most helpfully the statement of a layman who said that he became aware of his lack of any real "grounding in Christian beliefs," and that to be an intelligent, thinking Christian called for study—"not spasmodic attendance at occasional lectures, but regular, disciplined study beginning with the Bible." He pointed out, "How easy it is [and how insidious!] to mix together one small portion of Christ's teaching and a large measure of one's own selfish philosophy and thus become a disciple of the status quo, or of rationalized self-interest, or of a special class or race or nationality, all in the guise of 'following Christ.' "[4]

How very true! Those who bend the Christian teaching to fit their race prejudice or greed for money, or desire for status will do it violence. And those who stop with mere study and theory will do it equal violence.

God has called us to be seekers after truth. This is a lifetime endeavor. To get stalled on a few ideas, even though they are true, or to crystalize on a creed is to die intellectually and spiritually. As Nels F. S. Ferre has said, "The heart of the creeds may very well be true; they may point in the right directions; but they work to kill living faith. Only rugged personal faith can keep from being choked by creeds."[5] Firsthand religion calls for firsthand quest and fresh thought, a kind of eager and trembling anticipation. "Blessed are they which do hunger and thirst after righteousness: for they shall be filled" (Matt. 5:6). Expository, biblical preaching plus personal quest and obedience will produce a strong church—a people being constantly renewed, inspired, and strengthened. But both are necessary.

Third, genuine worship is essential if the church is to be constantly renewed. When the Word speaks to us clearly we soon feel our great need of divine grace. We feel our lack. We confess our failures. We find a cleansing. Ralph Sockman expressed it well. "To worship is to quicken the conscience by the holiness of God, to feed the mind with the truth of God, to purge the imagination by the beauty of God, to open the heart to the love of God, to devote the will to the purpose of God."[6]

True worship is not a smug, comfortable feeling. It is a cleansing which comes of honesty and contrition. It can relieve fear, anxiety, and tiring conflicts and bring calm only as there is a frank facing of need. It can bring us new and fresh perspective to see small or great matters for what they are so that we get our "bearings" again. It can, if we are honest, lead us to accept new disciplines in our living, and discipline leads to discovery.[7]

True worship will intensify our devotion to the cause of Christ and help us to avoid exaggeration of our problems. It will help us to be less critical and judgmental of other people as we see our own failures. It will help us to see how small we are and how great God is and so lead us to a greater dependence and faith in him. Meaningful worship will make us more sensitive to people, more aware of their hurts.

No wonder Jesus emphasized worship as something that is a reality, not tied to a certain place or form but "in spirit and truth" (John 4:23). Worship should never be merely a formality. It is not necessarily attached to any particular form or style, and the form or style cannot produce it whether you sing fast or slow, loud or soft; whether the pulpit is at one side of the chancel or in the center. How we *need* genuine worship for spiritual renewal.

Fourth, the church is renewed by the Holy Spirit. Jesus spoke of him as the "helper" or "comforter" or "counselor" (words used in different translations). He taught us that the Holy Spirit would teach, lead, reprove, convince, convict, and empower his people (see John 14, 15, 16). He promised that the Holy Spirit would make his followers able to witness to his saving power.

A witness, of course, is one who speaks from firsthand experience, and the Holy Spirit seems most at work when one life engages another life in the living and meaningful encounter of sharing in love. He is present as one dares to go out beyond his own known abilities and the safety zone of what is easy and familiar. He invites us to dare, to undertake, to test our sense of his guidance.

When we consider that the church is intended to be a responsive people sensing what God is doing in the world, then we can appreciate the very significant role and ministry of the Holy Spirit. How different this concept is from that which views Christianity and the church in rigid, fixed, institutional, and traditional terms—a loyalty that looks backward. Our conception is of the church as the continuing work of God as he creates and renews, redeems and heals, through the ministry of his people. If the church is to move with God at the cutting edge of progress, it will be by the enlightening, sensitizing, empowering presence of the Holy Spirit. That is renewal.

Fifth, renewal comes through meaningful relationships with one another as well as with Christ. We belong to Christ by belonging to one another. Whether we particularly like each other is not really the question. We can learn from each other and be thus renewed just because of a genuine relatedness in Christ and in his cause. Even a divergence of view can be a learning and growing experience, that is, if it is used constructively.

Fellowship is not necessarily perfect agreement or conformity to the same patterns or ideas. It is more likely disagreements in creative tension. It is the spirit and attitude which makes a disagreement the opportunity for contribution rather than conflict. Where everyone thinks alike, no one is thinking very much. It isn't our differences that present the greatest danger. It is the indifference. If we dare not disagree, then we dare not think or speak. The result will be a suppression of thinking, quenching of enthusiasm, absence of real involvement, and a deadening conformity. That is what has happened in many congregations.

On the other hand, if Christians speak out in harsh and judgmental fashion the effect is about the same—or worse! The effect of that is intimidation and fear. Freedom of expression is essential if a church is to be responsive to many needs as we become aware of them, and if it is to express the concerns, the competence, and the sense of vocation of its people. The church is people under God.

The object of the church should be to strive for such openness to one another and regard for one another that we can think with integrity, express ourselves with freedom (in the right spirit and attitude), learn from one another, sense God's will together, and unite in a real sense of mission.

This is possible only as we become objective enough and loving enough to respect one another as persons and as Christians, even when we differ. We achieve nothing when we hurry to smooth over every little rough spot and paper over the cracks in the plaster. The solution lies deeper. It is in the honest sharing of viewpoints, and sometimes agreeing to disagree. If we can accept one another without being judgmental, hear a viewpoint objectively, trying to understand, then we will find ourselves being renewed personally as well as corporately.

Sixth, renewal comes through a personal, genuine faith. There ought to be at the foundation of one's life a sense of encounter with the living God, the awareness of personal need, the confession of sin, the assurance of faith, the sense of vocation. This becomes deeply personal. It relates to one's own experience, to his own inner thought and his uniqueness as a person. No two persons are alike. God's plan for his people is unity in diversity, the unity which not only recognizes but fosters and encourages uniqueness. Christian unity is individuality supported by mutuality. It is the full flowering of the potential in each person and the full expression of each one's sense of vocation in a supportive and loving fellowship. Each of us is to be a growing person, encouraged and renewed by our life together.

Seventh, the church is renewed by being united in service and mission. We have observed earlier that the nature of the church is mission. We will not be renewed by blowing on our hands (or sitting on them). We will be renewed as we obey. There is only one place at which genuine spiritual renewal can take place and that is the point at which the church's *mission* in the world is being *fulfilled,* in its open and courageous *encounter* with *people* in the spirit of love. If it attempts to be a separate entity it will lose, not gain, its essential life and power, for its real life is the love of God flowing through it into the world. The new life in Christ has its very reality, its center and manifestation in everyday life. Renewal comes through servanthood.

TALK BACK

1. Do you discern any signs of renewal now in progress in your congregation? What are they? Are there signs of decay?

2. What percent of the people of your church are actively involved in its work? How do you see the reasons or factors leading to this?

3. Do you feel free to do your own thinking? To express your ideas? Do you feel that you are heard when you speak?

Study Activity

Send a committee to talk with a neighboring pastor for purposes of comparing the features of congregational life and morale. Find out how they do things, how they are organized. Then have them report on the relative strength and weakness they see.

---

[1] From the Bonebrake Theological Seminary *Bulletin,* 1948, Autumn issue.

[2] Bennett Cerf in *The Life of the Party.*

[3] Wallace E. Fisher, *Preaching and Parish Renewal* (Nashville: Abingdon Press, 1966), p. 17.

[4] Robert A. Raines, *Reshaping the Christian Life* (New York: Harper and Row, 1964), pp. 130, 131.

[5] Nels F. S. Ferré, *The Sun and the Umbrella* (New York: Harper and Row, 1953), p. 63.

[6] Ralph W. Sockman, *The Higher Happiness* (New York: Abingdon Press, 1950).

[7] See Albert Edward Day's *Discipline and Discovery* for an excellent treatment of this thought.

Chapter 8

The Responsive Stance

Attitude" is a key word. And in the space age it has taken on again its fuller meaning. It means disposition, feeling, or tendency as we know. But more, it means position or posture. In aeronautics attitude means the position of the aircraft relative to wind and ground. In any case, it means posture or stance as well as emotional disposition and there is a close relationship between the two.

When we say a person was "sitting on the edge of his chair" we mean he was alert, eager, and interested. If he was leaning back you would assume that he was not very interested. In this chapter, we are concerned with the attitude of readiness, that is, the *responsive stance*. Like runners on their mark before the race begins!

Jesus had a great deal to say about attitudes. Among the most quoted of all his sayings are the "beatitudes" (that word means a state of blessedness or happiness) in which he spoke of the conditions of mind and heart that make possible true happiness. The Sermon on the Mount (Matt. 5, 6, 7) is a compilation of Jesus' teachings which deal so much with one's attitudes, his set of mind, his openness to real meanings. He made it quite clear that we do not find satisfaction by seeking the approval of people or by living for material things, but rather by a condition of *being*. God does indeed call us into *being!* He himself was being in the highest sense. Paul Tillich once wrote,

When the apostles say that Jesus is the Christ, they mean that in Him the new eon which cannot become old is present. Christianity lives through the faith that within it there is the new which is not just another new thing but rather the principle and representation of all the really new in man and history. But it can affirm this only because the Christ deprived Himself of everything which can become old, of all individual and social standing and greatness, experience and power. He surrendered all these in His death and showed in his self-surrender the only new thing which is eternally new: love. . . .

"Love never ends," says His greatest apostle. Love is the power of the new in every man and in all history. It cannot age; it removes guilt and curse. It is working even today toward new creation. It is hidden in the darkness of our souls and of our history. But it is not completely hidden to those who are grasped by its reality.[1]

That's it: to be grasped by reality! But that is not a passive or neutral state. It is an exciting dimension of living.

What is the stance or posture of the church? Too often it is one of passivity and traditionalism. Much has been said about this in recent years but perhaps Halford Luccock said it as well as any.

One of the real dangers of Christianity . . . is that a backward looking nostalgia—a sentimental longing to go back and restore a familiar day that has either gone or never really existed—may be substituted for an ethical and spiritual religion. Nostalgia is a self-protective device which constantly recurs in times of crisis as a defense against the painful horrors of thinking. It is an alluring, though futile, attempt to escape the perplexities of an upset world, rather than face the demanding task of taking basic Christian principles into the contemporary world.[2]

Grow or die is a law of nature. It is true of all living things. It is true of the church. There is something very comfortable—and very deceptive—about the familiar. It feels good. It brings back a host of precious memories. It is associated with that which we hold even sacred. But watch out! About the best preserved thing in history is an Egyptian mummy!

The dangers we face today are like those common even in the days of the apostles. The Apostle Paul, writing under divine inspiration, called the churches of his day to rediscover what was vital. "Be not conformed . . . but be transformed," he cried, "that you may prove what is . . . the will of God" (Rom. 12:1, 2). We have to be always on guard against crystallizing into habitual forms. "Have an instinct for what is vital," Paul urged. That's the stance for the church.

Why is it that the identity of the church and its cohesion as a body are so tied to a place, a building, a time on Sunday morning, and to certain things we do at that time and place? Of course certain facilities are necessary to carry on religious work, just as they are necessary to carry on business or anything else. But our mission is among people! What shall we do about the people barred from decent housing or confined to servile jobs? How can we reach those who have never heard the gospel? What is it that has priority?

What is our stance? To what are we *responding,* if anything? The absence of any building or facility would not insure a responsiveness or care for people. But is our sense of identity really Christian? We are to follow Christ and express his concern for man. If we turn from that to material priorities and worldly prestige we make a radical departure from the Christian standard and the church becomes a montage of little idols.

Learning to Listen

"He that hath ears to hear, let him hear," cried Jesus (Matt. 11:15). But really very few heard. Only a few paid serious attention to his words, thought them through, and conscientiously tried to obey. The majority of the people followed him for a time and then headed back home. Others seemed to be there only to receive what physical help they needed or have a part when food was provided on that gentle slope of the hillside near the Sea of Galilee. "Will you also turn away?" he once asked a few followers. Not many shared his purpose. Always it has been that way.

Halford Luccock once spoke of "the aristocracy of the attentive," those who could see and hear and "who could give heed closely enough and long enough to discern the realities of which life gave evidence."[3] Then he went on to say that "Jesus rejected the common forms of aristocracy which the world accepted, aristocracies of birth or power or privilege." He turned to those who could open their minds and hearts to the fresh revealing of reality and life. There's the real "aristocracy" in any age!

Dr. Moffatt translated the words of Jesus in Matthew as he quoted from the prophet Isaiah. "You will hear and hear but never understand, you will see and see but never perceive. For the heart of this people is obtuse, their ears are heavy of hearing, their eyes they have closed, lest they see with their eyes and hear with their ears." Then Jesus added a word of commendation to those who were hearing him: "But blessed are your eyes, for they see, and your ears, for they hear!" (13:14b-16).

Real hearing and seeing call for a kind of internal receiving equipment. Someone spoke of the difficulty of conveying the aroma of a flower show by radio! No equipment to receive!

My wife and I went, one memorable evening, to hear a world renowned harpist. She was great. The concert hall was filled with glorious music. But in front of us sat a diminutive and resentful little man who had manifestly been brought there. His wife, a determined looking soul, sat rigidly beside him. The man fidgeted, twisted, and suffered through it. The music was there but it never got through to him. It was doubtful that much got through to the wife either, but she apparently was determined to get some culture and to see that he got some. He had no "ears to hear."

One reason Jesus has baffled the scholars of the world, both in ancient and modern times, is the fact that he brought living truths to people by the process of spiritual birth rather than by the rational process alone. "Except a man be born again," he said, "he cannot see the kingdom of God" (John 3:3). Or again, "Except ye be converted, and become as little children, ye shall not enter into the kingdom of heaven" (Matt. 18:3). As children? Yes. Have you ever seen the look of utter openness and eagerness on a child's face? No pretense. No mask. Just complete honesty.

It was after Jesus had sent out the seventy to preach and they had returned rejoicing over the success they had had that Jesus prayed, "I thank thee, O Father, Lord of heaven and earth, that thou hast hid these things from the wise and prudent, and hast revealed them unto babes" (Luke 10:21).

Wayne Oates has spoken of a "disciplined naiveté"[4] —a simplicity which means not the opposite of the profound but the opposite of duplicity or guise, a certain fresh and childlike eagerness and openness. He pointed out the importance of skill and knowledge with the unpretentious and childlike openness to learning in the realm of human and spiritual understanding. Christianity is more than facts we learn and things we do. It is a *moral* demand which requires decision. It is when we commit ourselves to Christ that the truth he taught comes alive within us.

Listening—for What?

What is the church *listening* to? To what is it *responding?* Before Christians can respond differently we must change our stance to one of responsiveness. If we hear only the voices of money and power—or the clamor of our own ambitions for social acceptance, we shall not respond to Christ. What are our objectives? Do we have any, really? How Christian are they?

There are the voices from the world and life about Christians today; the voices of harsh reality as the people around us have to live it. For many there is heartache and pain, loneliness and despair. For large numbers there is injustice and discrimination. They cry out in many ways. The haunted look on their faces is in itself a mute cry for someone to help.

Those who are caught in the economic trap as industry makes radical changes need help. They cannot always help themselves. Those who are caught in the deplorable living conditions of crowded tenement houses, unsafe and unsanitary, need help to break through the power structures to effect a change. They cry for help. Do we in the church have ears to hear?

To cultivate a sense of the spiritual without an awareness of human reality is somehow false. It doesn't follow Christ. No one ever heard the voices around him more clearly than Jesus Christ. And no one ever heard the voice of God as he did. The two are not incompatible. They belong together. The prophets heard the voice of God but in relation to the conditions and needs of their time. They became real reformers, social reformers, because they were in touch with God and with life. If the church is considered unimportant by many in today's world it is likely because it has been out of touch.

And that is just what is as dangerous as it seems comfortable. We rest in the feeling that all is well, that the turmoil in the world around us will go away and everything will return to normal. But what is normal? Are inequality and discrimination and injustice normal? Shall we close our ears to the cry for help? At the end of World War I a treaty was signed in Versailles, France. Lloyd George of England was exultant. It was a victorious day. The German army had been sliced down to a mere 100,000 men and its armament destroyed. Military training on any sizable scale was prohibited. The German navy had been reduced to almost nothing, and its personnel limited to 15,000 men. The German mercantile shipping had been given over, too. The German colonies had been given up. The idea was to secure a lasting peace, and the complete squelching of the war enemy seemed the way to do it.

But a little reflection on the part of historians teaches us that right there, in crushing a proud people, the soil was prepared and the seeds planted for World War II. Are those who sit on top of the heap really so victorious? Look again! The fire could be already burning quietly, ready to consume the victors. Those who feel victorious are often in great peril.

We Hear Calls for Help

The organized church has by and large represented the privileged class of people—the prosperous middle class. Even many conservative and evangelical groups that started among the less privileged are now properly counted middle class and fairly prosperous. The WASP (White, Anglo-Saxon, Protestant) designation is not altogether inappropriate. The deprived and disinherited are hardly welcomed—at least they wouldn't feel welcome. So we who make up the church are pretty well on top of the heap, too. Do you hear any crackling sounds of fire burning? "He that hath ears to hear. . . ."

The clamor among nominal Christians too much fills our ears. You have to get away to hear the voices of need. How very much we are absorbed with internal churchly activities. That seems to occupy most of our time and energy. To be democratic, to work together cooperatively, we have to make decisions together. But somehow, we don't get beyond the talking stage. When the priest and the levite Jesus told about "passed by" the unfortunate man by the roadside, they were most likely on some official religious business (maybe on their way to a committee meeting). It is the preoccupation of the church with itself and its many social activities unrelated to any real kingdom work that robs it of real ministry. Pastors are so driven by the demands of many involvements that they hardly have time for people in real need.

Taylor Caldwell has reminded us of our inability to hear what people are saying and of the great need of people just to be heard with love and understanding. She speaks about the clamor of churches themselves which makes it difficult for even the pastor to be a real listener.

> Our pastors would listen—if we gave them the time to listen to us. But we have burdened them with tasks which should be our own. We have demanded not only that they be our shepherds but that they take our trivialities, our social aspirations, the "fun" of our children, on their weary backs. We have demanded that they be expert businessmen, politicians, accountants, playmates, community directors, "good fellows," judges, lawyers, and settlers of local quarrels. We have given them little time for listening, and we do not listen to them, either.[5]

What does this say about the stance of the church? How much can the ear of your pastor be turned to people in need? How much of the interest and energy, the time and money, of your congregation is turned inward to your own enjoyment, and how much outward to the church's mission? Do the people of your congregation have any clear notion of what that mission is? Why not take a little survey to find out?

Just ask each person this question: What do you think our congregation should do (accomplish) in the next five years? (If the answers are vague or if you encounter blank stares, it should tell you something.) Tabulate the answers, listing the major goals suggested, the don't-know responses, the vague, general responses that mean little. Then, set up a conference with your pastor and see what goals he has in mind. Compare the results.

Fortunately, increasing numbers of churches are growing more sensitive to the calls for help that come from outside their walls. They are learning more about listening. They grow in sensitivity to need. They learn how to act out of a responsive stance. Some congregations have made it a definite part of their minister's responsibility—or have even added staff members for this purpose—to sharpen the congregation's activities in outreach in the community. Not that the paid staff is to do this work. It is to facilitate the work of people in the congregation.

And so they teach classes in jails and reformatories, help in detention homes, work in centers for poverty-stricken families. They tutor children to help them catch up in school. They get in dialogue with students on neutral ground outside church and school. They offer emergency help through telephone ministries and in other ways. They get active in clubs for children and youth. They sponsor parolees. All this and many other such things they do strongly in the name of Christ. They do it because they are aware, listening, standing in a responsive stance.

TALK BACK

1. Where do you find the most exciting challenges, in your work, your play, or your worship? What relationship do you see between your occupation and your Christian commitment?

2. History shows that the future belongs to the lean, disciplined, purposeful people, that the disciplined minority gains control. Can your church qualify for that?

3. In which situation do you feel the most at ease?

    (a) At a class party or social function.

    (b) In a class discussion.

    (c) In a prayer or quest group.

    (d) In a Sunday worship service.

    (e) Among people on the job (office, factory, etc.).

    (f) At the office party.

How do you analyze yourself in the light of your response?

Study Activity 1

Have group leaders list all the activities of their groups (study, worship, service projects), and the approximate amount of time spent in each. Then estimate how much of the effort is inward, how much outward.

Study Activity 2

Divide your study group into two parts. Let one part prepare a list of needs: some big ones drawn from the world scene, some major local problems, some individual concerns. Let the other part first suggest among themselves some general principles for responding to need. Then as they hear from the other part about certain needs, have them suggest ways the church and individual Christians may respond to them. The first part can, in turn, decide how adequate they feel the suggested responses are. This also can be related to next week's session.

[1]Paul Tillich, *The Shaking of the Foundations* (New York: Charles Scribner's Sons, 1948), p. 186.

[2]Halford Luccock, *Marching Off the Map,* p. 101.

[3]Ibid, p. 49.

[4]Wayne Oates, *The Holy Spirit in Five Worlds* (New York: Association Press), p. 66ff.

[5]Taylor Caldwell, *The Listener* (New York: Doubleday & Co., Inc., 1960), p. 10.

Chapter 9

The Responding People

On your mark. Get set. Go!" The two instructions at the first are preparation for the "Go." Whatever we may say about the responsive stance, it must be preparation to become *responding people*. The awareness will soon dim if we don't act. The preparation will be a mockery unless we do that for which we have prepared. The runner on his mark, all set, would be a ludicrous sight if the starting gun were never fired or if he failed to hear it. (How would you like to hold such a position all day?)

Obedience in Christian Action

Of course, it is possible to run around in circles and never get in the real race. Activism can be a frantic substitute for anything purposeful and directed. Just as a neurotic may, by incessant and trivial chatter, cover over the deep isolation and loneliness he feels, so can the busy activist in religion substitute for a living faith and make himself believe he is relevant.

The old controversy over faith and works, by trying to determine which one is really important, forgets that they are like two oars with which you row a boat. Use either alone and you go around in a circle. The pendulum seems to swing between the other worldly and this worldly emphases, between the individual gospel and the social gospel. Religious periodicals or interdenominational bodies may champion only one or the other.

When will we learn to take our Lord seriously and simply let the gospel say what it says? There is no individual or social gospel. There is only the *gospel*. There is no substitute for faith, and there is no substitute for obedience. Right here we are concerned with the obedience, the Christian *action*. While we hope to be delivered from what Vernon A. Lowscher calls "sentimental inertia"¹ we hope also, by God's wisdom, to be saved from "beating the air."

In the World

According to the notable prayer of Jesus for his people, the church is to be *in* the world but not *of* it, yet sent *into* it (John 17:15-19). What does this mean? The church is in society. It is a part of society and, to some degree, the product of society. Church and society are interacting, influencing and being influenced. The church is the product of God's redemptive work in Christ. Thus it is intended to live and perform in different terms and by different criteria or standards. It is not, therefore, *of* the world in spirit and purpose, but it is *in* the world as its sphere of responsibility and mission. Indeed every part of life on earth is a part of its mission. The whole gospel for the whole person in all his relationships—that is the goal. And the whole fellowship—the whole people of God—is needed.

The word *world* is used in different ways in the Bible. First, in the material sense, referring to the earth. Second, in the social sense, referring to the whole of mankind. Third, in the moral sense, referring to the corrupt and evil influences which grip mankind. It is with the social and moral meanings that we are concerned here. The church is in the world (in the social sense) but not of the world (in the moral sense).

We are to be people vibrantly present in the world of people, sensitive to the needs and hungers around us but we are to be so "present" with an integrity of life and a clear scale of values which is different from the commonly accepted patterns and standards of society. Failure to make distinctions in our use of words sometimes leads us into confusion. In this confusion the "world" has been rejected by many Christian people.

Stated briefly, involvement in the world without integrity of life and sound conviction can lead to defeating compromise. Integrity of Christian conviction and purpose without involvement in the world amounts to isolation. But integrity with involvement equals witness. If we learn this well we can move into our society with effectiveness. There are cries from both extremes.

Some would eliminate from Christianity all its genuinely "spiritual" (other-worldly) characteristics and discard any piety or evangelism. They would simply involve themselves with social change on the assumption that this alone will bring in the Kingdom. Others would have nothing to do with that but simply preach the gospel to convert individuals and "snatch brands from the burning." Which is it? Take a response from your class or discussion group to see what the viewpoint is.

On the Offensive

The church of the first century was not a group of self-consoling, self-conscious people in a kind of spiritual rest home. They thought of themselves then as engaged in a cosmic, life-and-death struggle with demonic forces. They wrestled "not against flesh and blood, but against principalities, against powers, against the rulers of the darkness of this world, against spiritual wickedness in high places" (Eph. 6:12). No wonder they needed the "whole armor of God."

Somehow we seem to have lost that sense of engagement with the real issues. In the last few years we have again heard and seen a strong emphasis on that aspect of the church's responsibility, but unfortunately that emphasis is sometimes associated with social action alone.

The most effective social change, however, is to be seen when the grace of God has effected change in individual lives and when such change is followed by obedience. John and Charles Wesley are remembered not only for the tremendous evangelistic impact they made upon England but also for the profound change produced in the whole of society in that land. They went to the people in open air meetings—a strategy learned from George Whitefield —and thousands were converted. They worked, not in rejection of the Anglican church, but outside its rigid structures. England was changed.

"Now it is true that the Christian faith is not primarily concerned with the establishment of a better social order, or even with the world as such, but with man's relationship to God and eternity. But the very nature of this faith in God, which is a mysterious gift of his grace, drives man back to the world of humanity which God loves and in Christ seeks to save."[2] There's the nub of it! Christianity that doesn't begin with the individual, *doesn't begin.*

But Christianity that ends with the individual, *ends.* "It is significant that in the Bible every encounter with the living God, from Moses to Paul, leads the individual to lose himself in the continuing redemptive activity of God among men."[3] He who taught us, "You must be born again," also taught us that we will be rejected at last if we do nothing to help "the least of these"—the hungry, the imprisoned, the naked, the stranger.

The church is intended to be on the offensive. Jesus declared that he would build his church and "the gates of hell shall not prevail against it" (Matt. 16:18). While "gates" is changed to "powers" in some translations, the meaning relates to defense. Gates in the great walls of the cities of that time were heavy iron or bronze, bolted and secured against invaders. It seems, then, that the church is to mount an offensive against the forces of death. The neutral church can hardly be called His church.

Witness to the Whole World

Aside from social action as such, we recognize that the primary purpose of the church is to bring to the whole world the witness of what God has done. It is the witness itself, not the results, which is our perpetual business. If we become primarily concerned with results or success we will be in grave danger of substituting our own designs and efforts for that which is authentically scriptural and Christian. Human contrivance can get results that are less than Christian. To be effective we have to accommodate our approach in order to communicate the gospel. We need not accommodate the gospel itself. If we do, we achieve only synthetic success.

In all this we apply general ethical and scriptural principles to particular problems of conscience or conduct. We deal with less-than-ideal conditions, and, for that matter, less-than-ideal people—even in the church. If we are devastated and disillusioned because of difficulties in applying our lofty ideals, we shall soon quit, discouraged.

Jesus was faced with this problem. Some questions put to him went unanswered. Some problems of a philosophical and theological nature he did not discuss. He simply portrayed, in his person, his conduct, and his teaching, the nature and love of God. He did not give us neat little rules and regulations to go by. He did not answer all our questions. As a matter of fact he might have raised some questions! Our task is not greater than his. There are some things we don't know (for instance, why do good people suffer?). But we have a witness to bear. We are custodians of the fact of God's self-disclosure in Christ.

That is enough. On the one side of our coin are etched the words, "I don't know," but on the other side, "I believe."

Witness is the word. Not lawyer or judge but simply witness. We do not pose as experts. We do not profess to know all or to be all. We confess that Jesus Christ is Lord as well as Savior, and, as witnesses to what God has done, we live with him on the moving frontier. "We have this treasure in earthern vessels, that the excellency of the power may be of God, and not of us" (2 Cor. 4:7). We are the custodians of his mighty act.

As human beings, we assume a risk when we tackle the tasks of the kingdom, when we engage the powerful, entrenched evil of the world. How can you be sure you will come out on top and be successful? You can't! How can you be sure, in this complex, interdependent, intermeshed society that you have the answer? You can't! You take the risk. But if you withdraw from the conflict in fear, then relevance is impossible. Do we, then, have a choice? Thank God, he is on his throne. Our challenge is to sense what he is doing in our day and cooperate with him as best we can know his will.

It will help us immensely if we recognize that we are part of the human situation and, in the very nature of that fact, share in the responsibility (even guilt) for the conditions. We need to rejoin the human race. Indeed, just because we are Christians, our responsibility becomes all the greater. We are, by that fact, thrust into the unfinished work of our Lord, as co-workers with him. Just because we are his, we respond to need in his name. The need itself becomes the call. As the prophets of Israel identified themselves with the backslidden condition of their people, confessing for them; as Paul agonized for his people, willing to take upon himself their guilt (Romans 9:3); so we recognize our oneness with mankind. The church is "separated unto the gospel" but not separated from the world of people.

The Mission Dimension

Thus, the identity of the church is in its mission and message, not in an isolated existence, not in the monastery but in the marketplace. We tend to identify the church with a place or a time on Sunday. But the church scattered throughout the community on Tuesday afternoon at two o'clock is no less valid than when it is gathered for worship at eleven o'clock on Sunday morning. There must be the inbreathing and outbreathing of worship and work, of learning and sharing, of renewal and witness.

Worship has great meaning for those who have obeyed in mission, and real mission becomes possible and effective only as we have met God in worship. Our preaching is hollow and empty if not accompanied by living witness. No country would require its army's generals to go out and fight its battles while the great army of soldiers stood on the sidelines as spectators. Yet much of the church expects this kind of thing. Church members "want to stand at a safe distance and watch their gladiator perform. If he scores victories they will cheer; if he wavers they will cut down their subscription."[4]

Equipped to Serve

According to the Ephesian letter, the purpose of teaching and pastoral care is to "equip God's people for work in his service" (4:12, NEB). It is for the maturing and development, the strength and resources necessary to be effective Christians. When a person engages life and need he soon feels his need of worship and strength. Those who feel no need for worship are manifestly not engaged in anything significant, not even in Christian growth. Far from relevance or involvement being separated from worship, it is deeply related to worship. When we question the ingrownness of the church we are not challenging the validity of real worship, but the opposite—we are saying that real worship *grows out* of obedience and servanthood.

Servanthood is related to both individual and group action. A major part of making any appreciable difference in life and society about us will have to be borne by individual witness and work but the church as a body also makes its presence and witness felt. It is a prophetic community with a prophetic message, not reflecting conditions but reflecting the will and purpose of God; not speaking out of the situation but out of eternal values *to* the situation. "For the time is come that judgment must begin at the house of God" (1 Peter 4:17).

The church as an institution stands for something. It offers support, hopefully, to those who represent it in the marketplace or legislative assembly. If a Christian is to be involved in public affairs, if he is to be more than a spectator, if he is to get into the arena of conflict, he will of necessity deal with issues provisionally, with situations and conditions that are less than ideal, indeed sometimes downright nasty!

Jesus was crucified because he dared to engage the vested interests and entrenched evil in a moral struggle. He took the initiative in doing that. He made it clear that we, too, bear a cross. There are at work today evil forces which shape or destroy thousands of lives and homes. The liquor industry, the tobacco industry, the narcotics racket, the peddling of pornography, the unjust system that keeps thousands of our citizens in bondage and poverty while they are denied the freedoms guaranteed by our Constitution—all these and more have had an almost free hand in exploiting people. Will they go unchallenged while we have our inspiring worship services and console ourselves?

That's where we have often forsaken the gospel. We piously finger our crosses (in gold, of course) and mumble meaningless phrases but manage never to get ourselves crucified.

To be a responding people means to respond to God by serving people and to respond to people in terms of what God has, through Christ, done in the world. As he was "sent into the world" so he has sent us into the world.

TALK BACK

1. Have someone in your group bring a report on the effect of John and Charles Wesley's ministry in English society in the eighteenth century. Compare it with today's situation.

2. Can the church of today reach the vast majority of people with its present structures and methods? What changes, if any should be made?

3. Can a person be a vital Christian and engage in politics? Are any of your congregation so involved? What is your congregation's reaction? Would such a person generally be able to bring about a genuinely Christian solution to the problems he faces?

4. To what extent do we as Christians have to share the guilt for injustice and denial of freedom to less privileged people?

5. "We cannot do everything at once," said Calvin Coolidge, "but we can do something at once." What?

Study Activity

Take a survey among the people of your congregation to see how many are engaged in some form of community work or social service. Then evaluate the responsiveness of your congregation.

---

[1]Vernon A. Lauscher, "Sentimental Inertia" *The Pulpit* (September, 1968), pp. 22-24.

[2]*The Asbury Seminarian* (January, 1967), p. 25.

[3]*Ibid.*

[4]David Dawson, *More Power to the Church* (Grand Rapids: Zondervan Publishing House, 1940), p. 44.

Chapter 10

Responsible Leadership

If the Christian church is to rejoin its own revolution and express the radical and revolutionary new life in Christ, it needs leaders of the first order. Much of Christendom is like a great slumbering giant with potential strength but too long at plate and pillow. How can we wake the giant, stir him into action, direct his energies?

We have some eighty-three million Protestant church members in North America with only a small minority active in any real Christian service. That is not so much a reflection on the people as on the leadership, the program, the inward-looking, subjective mentality.

We seem bound to the outworn forms, the institutions and buildings which are sometimes more the extension of egos and pride than means of service in the kingdom of God. Only a bold and courageous leadership can change the condition, daring to cull out the deadwood and mobilize for mission.

Waiting for Leadership

The majority of people wait for leadership. They do not, of themselves, rise up and move together. This is true in the nation. While men will work hard for private gain, they will not, unless mobilized by strong leaders, work continuously for the public interest. They will vote pretty much in terms of the promises made by politicians and how they personally would be affected. Even the politician's previous performance may be forgotten and the glittering promises followed in the blind hope of getting more for oneself.

But whatever the motivation, a great many people are always ripe for the demagogue who feeds their prejudices, appeals to their selfish interests, whips up their latent hostilities, and offers them a plan of action. As the quality of leadership goes, so goes the nation. Do we not, then, need responsible Christians in public office? And do we not need prophetic leaders in the church?

While this perhaps should not be true in the church, it is for the majority of church members who simply follow a custom and subscribe to "religion-in-general." The church is always in need of renewal and revival. Constant and diligent effort is needed to enlist people in active Christian commitment and ministry. The church's ministry is a corporate ministry, a total participation, for God seeks to work through the whole body of his people.

The process of renewal necessarily means perpetual cleansing by casting off all extraneous elements as well as the constant building up of vital forces. The hope lies in courageous leadership and teaching, in disciplined people set not on the preservation of the status quo nor on the "sanctified stupidities"[1] of the past but on the building of a new order. This calls for keen thinking, sublime courage, and the ability to distinguish between the essentials of our faith and the accretions of culture or tradition.

Responsible leaders are able to make these distinctions and to lead the way. But often their most heartbreaking problem is that they are accused of betraying the very faith they cherish. No one can walk the new path, bring new vision, or reinterpret the task without bringing criticism upon his own head. The prophets were persecuted men. Sooner or later the bitter opposition of those who consider themselves to be guardians of the existing forms will turn against the progressive leader and reproach him. He has to endure the hard experience of being called a destroyer of the very cause he gives his life to build.

The task of responsible leadership is to maintain and foster a rich fellowship in the church without allowing it to become isolated. The best leadership produces fellowship in obedience to our Lord. We need not be ingrown in order to have a vital relationship with one another as Christians. The church is a covenant people—in covenant with God. We need the strong base of loving fellowship to sustain us as we engage in living dialogue and encounter with those who may be unconcerned or even hostile. The role of leadership within the church is a vital one, both for the nurture and preparation of the church and the engagement in its mission.

Goals of Leadership

Toward this end the Ephesian letter is written in part. After portraying in graphic and moving terms, God's mighty act through Christ, the Apostle speaks of the vocation (calling) of every Christian and how we ought to conduct ourselves in relation to one another. Then he speaks of God as he works through the whole body of his people, and the gifts of the Spirit as he equips and enables his people for service (Eph. 4:1-8, NEB). There were "some to be apostles, some prophets, some evangelists, some pastors and teachers" (v. 11). These were to be key leaders, all of them relating to teaching in one form or another. Manifestly, preaching and teaching are central and basic in the church. But there follows the listing of several objectives in this leadership, each one important.

First, these leaders were "to equip God's people for work in his service" (v. 12). The goal, mind you, is to fulfill the mission of the church, namely to extend through the succeeding ages the redemptive work of Jesus Christ. It is important to keep this viewpoint. The gifts of the Spirit are serving gifts. They are related to the equipping and enabling of his people for the fulfilling of their vocation. The special gifts listed (prophet, evangelist, apostle, pastor, or teacher) are not *all* the gifts but those necessary for the healthy functioning of the entire body.

Instead of equipping his people for real service the pastor sometimes is trapped by the demands of those who pay his salary. His time is absorbed by the church itself, for itself, and the true mission of the church is almost forgotten. The pastor himself has often either given up on his real task or never was aware of it. He may either try to succeed by performing before his spectator-parishioners or becoming a man-about-town on behalf of the institution (organization man). The church cannot fulfill its mission until the pastor sees his real function of equipping the people for that mission and has the courage to work accordingly.

Second, leadership is for "building up the body of Christ" (v. 13). This means, of course, the obedient people. Here again, teaching is implied. If we are to be effective in our mission we need to be spiritually prepared. If we are to live out Christ's love we need to receive his love constantly. If we are to feed others we ourselves need to be fed. Worship and instruction have great meaning in relation to the life of obedience.

Third, leadership is necessary in order to "attain to the unity inherent in our faith and our knowledge of the Son of God—to mature manhood . . . " (v. 13). There is a *given* unity which is simply a part of Christian experience. When two or more persons are born of the Spirit there is a basic unity inherent in their faith in Christ. But this given unity is to be kept in the "bonds of peace" (v. 3). Unity of the Spirit may be destroyed for lack of pastoral leadership, teaching, counsel, and care. When misunderstandings arise among people, leadership is needed.

Good pastoral leadership nourishes and sustains fellowship. The very zeal a dedicated Christian has for the kingdom's work may be a source of embarrassment and annoyance unless given guidance and kept in harmony with others. The church has a corporateness which is, in itself, a witness. Internal harmony is essential to the witness. "By this shall all men know that ye are my disciples, if ye have love one to another" (John 13:35). Most of the problems in a congregation could have been avoided if only time had been taken to understand, to counsel together, and work unselfishly. Leadership is crucial.

Fourth, leadership is given the responsibility to "speak the truth in love" so that the church might "grow up into Christ" (v. 15). The objective in all this is to produce a body of people who, individually and corporately, are responsive to Christ in what he is doing. They are to express his spirit, share his love, proclaim his message, witness to his power, and carry forward his redemptive ministry. It is the living presence of Christ that always corrects and guides us. It is his truth expressed through his faithful servant that helps us grow up in him.

The Nature of Leadership

But let us inquire further into the nature of leadership in the church. It is not the same as that of politics or business, though there may be some similarities. In business the leader image is of the hard driver, the tycoon with telephones ringing and secretaries or subordinates dashing in and out of his luxurious office. In politics he is the adroit manipulator, the powerful influence who can make or break men.

But in the church (in the New Testament sense at least) he is a person called by God in the midst of a company of people who also are called to Christian mission. His function is primarily to enlist, instruct, encourage, equip everyone for personal service. He guides God's people in their ministry to one another and to people outside the fellowship as they serve and witness.

One of the most unfortunate errors we have made is departing from, or at least neglecting, that principle of the church. The whole church is intended to be a ministry. The pastor who tries to supply all the needs and be the one who ministers to everybody, is tempted to be false by pretending to have answers and resources when he doesn't, and is robbing others whose experience and insight might be more helpful than his own.

He may be ever so wise, but if people come to depend on him they may remain stunted in their own growth. He may be very informed and knowledgeable but the goal is not for him to be the answer man. It is that each one of his people will become a mature Christian, standing on his own feet, thinking for himself, and being able to teach others. The very abilities of a leader can keep others immature if he allows himself to be indispensable. The objective is a mature people. This is the nature of leadership, then, that every person fulfill his own calling.

Everybody Leads

Furthermore, almost every person can be a leader in some area. If the leader insists on always being that, he may do violence to others in what they can do as well as or better than he. To tap resources of skill and experience in people he will encourage everyone to put his mind and heart to use in the kingdom. Take a survey in your class or group and see how many different skills and abilities are represented there. Then discuss how these might be related to Christian outreach and ministry. Might the salesman, for instance, know something about approaching people, getting and following up prospects, which would be applicable as you seek to reach new people for Christ? Do we inspire people to be their best, to use their abilities in real ministry? Or is our leadership such that it makes them dull? Is the pastor a key person in this sense?

I once read of a very rich man who ordered from abroad, at a very high price, a pair of faultless, highbred horses which he wanted to drive for himself. After a year or so the horses would not have been recognized for the fine animals they were. Their eyes were dull, their gait lacked style, and they were just ordinary.

Then he called in an expert hostler and coachman who drove them for a month or two. In that time they again held their heads proudly, their eyes once again sparkled with luster, their gait was one of precision and grandeur. It took the expert to drive them in accordance with the nature of the horse and an understanding of what it was to drive. The expert's secret was in bringing out the horses' own finest qualities.

A true leader is unselfish in that sense. He seeks to help every person realize his own highest usefulness. He may push other people forward. He will not lose by doing this but rather gain in leadership and usefulness. When he helps take the chains off somebody else, he will bind him to his own heart with loving hoops of steel. On the contrary, if he attempts to be always in the limelight, gaining recognition, he builds on sand. The nature of the church is such that its strength—and the strength of every person in it—lies in harnessing the genius, imagination, skills, and understanding of the "whole people of God."

The Farsighted Leader

The responsible leader is a farsighted person, a strategist—not in the sense of manipulating people but of thinking ahead, sensing the times, watching the trends, observing, studying, and reflecting. The prophets were men of great vision, keen insight, careful observation, and sublime courage. They spoke from divine inspiration but also from discipline and obedience.

Many people think of a prophet as one who foretold future events by some magical or miraculous power, as one who announced, without knowing why or how, some far-off event to come. But the mission of the prophet was also that of a religious patriot, a statesman with moral and spiritual insight, involved in the eternal nature of things. He was different from others, not because he lived in some sort of divine ecstasy all the time but because he had clearer, more thought-through convictions and the courage to proclaim them. His confidence arose out of the awareness of God, of truth, and of events.[2] He was a strategist in the best sense. It seems clear that the church needs more prophets now who can read and interpret the events of our time and speak the eternal truth.

In the coming years, the church, if it is to continue with any relevance, needs courageous and responsible leaders who will not be unbalanced by extremists but at the same time will challenge the status quo. There are serious fractures in society. There are serious problems of self-satisfaction in the church. There are radicals and revolutionaries. There are reactionaries and diehards. Where is the prophet? He is somewhere in the midst of all this with clear vision and courage to resist irrational extremes.

In a dispatch during World War I, the noted Marshall Foch reported: "Outflanked on the right; outflanked on the left. Situation on the whole excellent—am going to advance."[3] Can we find leaders who will spearhead fresh thrusts into enemy territory? It remains to be seen whether we can distinguish the prophetic voice amidst all the clamor of voices—and march into the exciting future.

The Making of Leaders

It takes more than a title, or clerical garb, or theological lingo to make one a leader. As a matter of fact, the true prophet and responsible leader may not fit into our churchly conceptions. Amos didn't. That herdsman from the rugged and severe hills of Tekoa looked like anything but a prophet—even he denied any pretense at being one—but God used him when the recognized leaders and priests were playing it safe with the power structures of their day. From his fresh viewpoint and out of a courage born of conviction and concern, he spoke the word of the Lord.

Every congregation, every individual Christian shares in the development of the leadership that is so much needed in being the community of Christian love. Where do we find candidates? They are all around, and they include everybody connected with the fellowship. Boys and girls may be helped to exercise leadership now and to grow up as leaders. Youth need the opportunity to exert leadership not just isolated in a youth group but throughout the whole congregation. Men and women of all walks of life, with all kinds of skills and abilities, and at all levels of accomplishment need to be encouraged to express their leadership.

This calls for the kind of church life and structure that enables people to participate widely, fully, deeply, with leadership roles constantly being shared. This calls for a rather continuous effort to develop leaders through courses and church activities that bring out initiative, responsibility, and creativity. Thus, for instance, an adult Sunday school class becomes a place where not just one person stands and talks to the rest of the group week after week. Instead, the participation is wide; leadership is shared. Opportunities for participating in planning and making key decisions related to service activities, the chance to share in these responsibly—all must be constantly provided.

In such practical and down-to-earth ways do we start down the road to that place where the church shows wise, strong, and glorious leadership that begins to meet the great needs of the world.

TALK BACK

1. Franklin Field said, "Poor eyes limit a man's sight. Poor vision limits his deeds." Do we have leaders with real vision in the church now? How do we compare, in that respect, with earlier leaders in our church? Are there any prophets?

2. Someone said that what we lack in vision someone has to furnish in super-vision! How much vision do we have? Are we willing to accept supervision? Will we have to rely on some supervisory structure to get on with the task?

3. Why are not more people actively engaged in God's work? Of the list below, which do you feel is the chief obstacle in your congregation? How can you get around it?

    a. People are too preoccupied with other things.

    b. There has been no training program to prepare them.

    c. Just a few people run the church and do the work.

    d. The people have never been challenged to do it.

    e. We have never had the concept of leadership as portrayed in this chapter.

Study Activity

Use No. 3 question above in taking a poll among adults of your church (include older youth). Report your findings to the group. Share them with your church leaders.

---

[1] Halford Luccock, *Marching Off the Map,* p. 9.

[2] Credit to Rufus Jones, *Spiritual Energies* (New York: The MacMillan Company, 1949), pp. 55, 56.

[3] *Quote* (March 12-18, 1950), p. 8.

Chapter 11

Cooperation
Without Compromise

Because of the testimony of one man who had been very deep in crime and who had been marked for death by others in a vast organization of criminals, we have had some inkling of the deep entrenchment of organized crime and how it is linked together. The name "Cosa Nostra" brings chills to our spines. All kinds of crimes in hundreds of communities are intertwined and linked together (with the consent of some crooked law enforcement officers). For years honest law enforcement agencies have tried to crack that organization but with only limited success. Even the sophisticated and effective Federal Bureau of Investigation has met with frustration. That illustrates the massiveness and complexity of evil.

The Problems Are Vast

We are deeply perturbed by the existence of great slum areas in our cities. How did they come to be? How can we meet the problem that costs our country many millions of dollars in fighting crime and disease and all the other malevolent results? How can we help the poor who live there? What can we do to change conditions where they must pay more for their food, where they are charged outlandish interest rates on every dollar they must borrow? Such questions immediately bring up a whole string of related questions. They involve banking, business, labor, marketing, management, and real estate as well as human relations. Who has the answer? What shall we do as the church?

Of course, there are some things we can do personally. And we should. But we deal so much with the results rather than the causes. It is good to extend Christian love to the narcotics addict but what about the indescribably evil racket that pushes narcotics and draws innocent and unsuspecting young people into its clutches? How can we get behind the scenes and tackle the cause? Powerful and ruthless criminals are aggressively seeking more wealth. It will take power and skill to change that.

If we Christians want to stop with having a good life for our families, maintaining a Christian standard for ourselves, then we can rest right where we are. But if we accept the fact that Christ calls us to help our fellowman, we are immediately led into some hard questions and deeply entrenched problems. In this complex, interdependent, intertwined society in which we live, a personal Christian conscience and personal Christian service—while very important and necessary—are just not enough. We must challenge the structures of society which rob people of their proper rights.

We Can't Do It Alone

But you can't do it alone. And your congregation can't do it alone, even in your own community. The job is too big. It requires massive strength, careful strategy, and expertise. It calls for information hard to obtain. But what an individual cannot do, or even one group cannot do, Christians united *can* do. If the church groups in your community work together to do what none of them alone can do, the result may be quite different. And if united action is undertaken, there surely will be conscientious people in government, in business, and in the professions who will pool their knowledge and contacts to help. Some of our conscientious public leaders are distressed over the divided condition of the churches and their apparent blindness to the need.

A judge in one town spoke of the pornography and obscenity on the newsstands. "Where," he asked, "are the Christian people of this community? Do they not know about this, or don't they care?" He wanted to do something but technicalities of the law tied his hands. I could cite hundreds of examples. Why don't churches cooperate to combat such evils? Well, many seem to be afraid to cooperate with others lest they somehow compromise their own convictions or standards. Is that valid? Is there any difference between cooperation and compromise?

In the face of evil powers which threaten humanity with misery and destruction many prejudices and animosities which divided Christians in the past seem less and less important. Largely in response to pressing social needs the "ecumenical" age of the church came into being. How can we obey God all alone? How can we relate helpfully to our communities and their people without finding some kind of working relationship with our fellow Christians? How can we portray the love of Christ if we cannot come to some degree of unity among ourselves as Christians? Thus, the united action of Christians is related both to the nature and magnitude of our task and to the effectiveness of our Christian witness.

In the great cities, this becomes absolutely essential if needed ministries are to be made available to the deprived, for they are not a part of your parish. They couldn't come if they would, and they wouldn't if they could. They live in a different world.

The Impulse Toward Christian Unity

An interesting thing is seen on the Christian frontiers in other countries. The impulse toward Christian unity sweeps like a tide in many lands. Much of its leadership and inspiration has been drawn from those most deeply concerned with the church's mission to serve and evangelize humanity. Many of the pace-setting achievements of cooperative action among Christians are to be found in these other countries of the world, where the magnitude of the task simply dwarfs into insignificance the things that divide the sending churches.

Ordinarily it is thought that this sort of thing is happening among the old, mainline church bodies and it is dubbed ecumenical. But it is happening on a massive scale among the distinctly evangelical and conservative groups as well. An example of this is seen in the Evangelism in Depth program under the Latin American Mission. Behind the scenes a great deal of united action has been taken. Major moves toward uniting have been seen in foreign lands, perhaps more significant than in the United States. The Church of South India would be a case in point. The task itself drives us to cooperation and the *mission* of the church brings new perspective upon the *nature* of the church.

"Ecumenical"—Pro and Con

It should be made clear that the ecumenical movement is not to be identified with any single one of its institutional expressions. The word *ecumenical,* of course, means universal or belonging to the whole inhabited world. It is really a movement of the Spirit and is not to be thought of as confined to any structure. There are countless expressions of it, from cooperation between or among Christian people in a community to the international relationships of denominations; from retreats and camps devoted to fellowship and learning to the structured work of various councils and federations or organizational merger of denominations. It is the mood of our time brought on to a considerable degree by the need for a united witness at the times and places where it has to be done with strength.

We can frankly face the dangers in the ecumenical movement. Perhaps the most dangerous is the "ecumaniac" mentality that believes it can do no wrong or pursues it as the popular thing. There is danger that cooperative work and organizational federation be confused with that unity which arises out of new life in Christ and results in a deep relationship the New Testament knows as koinonia. There is the danger of confusing conformity with unity. Simply to go along might well indicate shallowness rather than love or commitment. There is the danger of longing for something big and powerful, of seeking a mammoth organization for its own sake. Whatever we do, we ought to recognize that it is the mission of the church in obedience to Christ alone that shapes our life together. The church essentially is the people of God on mission.

Perhaps we are confused because we don't distinguish between cooperation and compromise. Many devoted Christian people are disturbed about the ecumenical movement. It has come to have for these people the overtone of compromise, liberalism, and shallow thinking. Doesn't one have to surrender his own convictions in order to participate? Much depends upon the individual involved.

If his convictions are few and his thinking shallow, then he will bring that condition to all of his relationships. If, on the other hand, he thinks seriously and if he is committed to sound convictions, he will not be swayed (or even embarrassed) in the presence of those who differ.

On the contrary he will bear a significant witness. Our real concern should be the shallow thinking for it will affect the church at every level. The sound, middle course, it seems, would be cooperative action and unique witness. Let the real Christian stand up and be counted. Let him speak his convictions with both clarity and charity.

If we wait until Christians are agreed on everything, we shall be waiting a long, long time. To go our separate ways with little or no communication accomplishes nothing. Prejudice grows. Suspicions increase. We judge one another with the flimsiest kind of knowledge and the most superficial impressions. One of the great values of the whole ecumenical movement has been that followers of Christ have begun to share views candidly, and we have been amazed at how much of the problem stems from misunderstanding.

There have been mutual study, conversation, and cooperation. This is one of the most dramatic and impelling developments in the history of the church, one that is worthy of our sincere prayers for God's direction. As John Wesley expressed vehemently his disapproval of "narrowness of spirit" and "party zeal" so we are distressed over the bigotry which makes many so unwilling to believe that there is any authentic work of God except among themselves.

Just to experiment, ask half a dozen people in your congregation what their convictions are about unity among Protestants and how they feel about your congregation engaging in cooperative Christian work in your community. Ask them about membership in your city association or council of churches or about cooperating in an evangelistic crusade. What are the guiding principles or convictions expressed? Are there any? How well have the members of your class, or the leaders of your church,

thought through these questions? If your church is not a part of the cooperative work, what is the real reason? Is it because of convictions? Or prejudice? Or just plain unconcern?

"What is the future of the small denomination in America?" asked one leader of a small denomination. He went on to say that if we are to take hold of the big and important issues, a great deal of numerical strength, monetary support, and professional skills would be necessary. He saw that his group could go on preaching, teaching, winning people to Christ, and carrying on what they were already doing. That was quite possible and presented no problem. But to try to go alone meant that they were really not doing their full duty.

They were not coming to grips with the involved problems which so affect community after community. He observed that fewer than fifty people own the principal channels of information in America, that some five companies own the movie-making industry which so shapes the thinking of youth, that four companies very nearly control the radio industry. He felt these syndicates of power are beyond our reach as churches unless we unite to bring a united voice representing enough people so that it will be heard. In that particular denomination they felt they had a significant heritage which they were unwilling to lose. They wanted to have a part in united action and at the same time bear their unique witness. Was his position sound? Can you cooperate in such ventures without compromising your standards?

What, Really, Do We Mean by Unity?

Some of us who have talked about unity are being asked just what we mean. We are invited to engage in serious dialogue. And who should be involved in such dialogue

more than the evangelical Christian with concerns for unity? He knows, both by the Bible and by his own experience, that unity of the spirit which is *given* and which is a part of the church in its very nature. He is aware that organizational union is useless if it is not grounded in scriptural experience. To speak and to be heard, to receive and to share, to ask questions and to answer when you can, ought to be considered an honorable and vital task. And at no place is that witness and presence more needed than in relation to social responsibilities.

Evangelical groups have allowed themselves to appear uninterested in social problems or in the needs of bodies and minds (only in the soul!). Historically that has not been true. In this country and in England especially, evangelical Christians worked together and with other interested citizens toward social reform. Slavery was ended in Britain, then in the United States. A better life was made for the laborer. The deprived and the needy were cared for. Working conditions were improved. Child labor was eliminated. Women gained the right to vote.

The social gospel movement that existed before World War II largely failed (though it did a great deal of good, too) because it thought of evil primarily as bad environment which had to be changed by social action. It is easy to overlook the fact that a bad environment is both a result of sin and a cause of sin. It's a vicious circle. No one should know better than one who has been born of God that Christian service comes naturally out of the regenerated life (though it surely must be cultivated) and has an impact upon both the individual and upon his environment.

Thus, both the concern for social justice and the concern for Christian unity should be very much in the hearts of evangelical Christians. The real issue is whether we have

the interest, the courage, and the convictions to enter into active engagement and bear our witness. Isolation (or insulation) is unthinkable in such a time as this. To be a responsive people—that is, to respond to human need, or to respond to God in what he manifestly is seeking to do in the world—means to sense our larger relationships in both Christendom and in the society around us.

Some groups reach out with sensitivity and awareness to their fellow Christians and they do it without compromising their convictions. Increasingly other Christians feel that to recognize the one God and Father surely means to recognize also that all Christians are brothers.

Diversity enriches us but dividedness robs us. Can we trust the Holy Spirit to teach us together? Dare we engage in creative venture and honest exchange? If we are afraid to do so, will it not reveal a good deal about *us?* How, in the complex, intertwined structure of society, can we hope to be effective if we react in fragmentary fashion, presenting a divided front, and making only vague gestures?

Of course there are some underlying misgivings and these may not be entirely without foundation. One is the fear of an overarching and dominant organization which will presume to speak for all Christians. And that may be if we do not make our own convictions known. Another is the fear of an alien ideology dominating the ecumenical scene (presumably through some council or interdenominational organization) and drowning out individual convictions. Yet, most of us can hardly say we have tested sufficiently to draw any conclusions.

And, too, there is more than one channel for interdenominational action. If the organized church of our day—or any part of it—is to be responsive to God and to human need; if it is to respond effectively to the powerful forces

which shape or destroy lives, we have a moral obligation to explore avenues of cooperative work.

Perhaps this will be, for the most part, in the social arena, leaving the teaching and worship to be carried out in the unique ways we deem necessary. Perhaps the specialized forms of ministry such as to deprived persons, to those in institutions, or in the armed forces must be done cooperatively. Perhaps church groups should do more in sharing of facilities and not tie up so much money in buildings to be used only a few hours each week. There may be many ways for Christians to become less denominational in their frame of thinking and devote more of their resources in service to people.

Talk Back

1. What separates your congregation from the others in your community? Is it your convictions? If so, what are they? What do you feel is unique about your congregation, your contribution, or your witness?

2. How much do you know about other church groups? about their people, their teaching, their ways of worship? At what points do you differ? Or agree?

3. Is your congregation at all active in cooperative work in your community? In what areas? Are there areas of cooperative work you decline to participate in? What are your reasons? (Perhaps you will want to invite your pastor to discuss this with you.)

Study Activity

Why not dispatch a person or two from your group to talk with key leaders in the interdenominational work of your community—and get a list of the objectives, the programs, and conditions for participation. Then report back.

Chapter 12

The Church of Tomorrow

Gilbert W. Stafford clarified our thinking about the nature of the church when he insisted upon its movemental nature.[1] He properly pointed out that "We are called to be aware of, to be sensitive to, and to participate in the divine movement of God." Then he went on to describe the nature of that movement as being (1) of *God* through Christ *to the world,* (2) of *God* through Christ *in the world,* (3) of *people* through Christ *to God,* (4) of *people* through Christ *to people,* and (5) of *people toward fulfillment.* Such a concept of the church in dynamic rather than static terms, as ministry rather than organization, as mission rather than institution, challenges many of our assumptions and sets us on the road of adventure.

The Church Does Have a Future

Then, what about the church of the future? Does the church *have* a future? Shall we believe those who say it is irrelevant, that its structure is obsolete and its thinking outdated? You wouldn't have to look far to find examples of that. On the other hand you can find examples of the church very much alive, relevant, and vital. It all depends.

It is interesting that the Judeo-Christian faith was initiated through a nomadic people—mobile and responsive to divine guidance in the wilderness. Their faith was not tied to a place. They moved as God moved them. They dwelt in tents. The tabernacle was a portable build-

113

ing or tent. Today again we are a kind of nomadic, moving people (only we have trailers). But after years of thinking in parish patterns—a place of worship, a time of worship, a highly organized life—many Christians find it difficult to capture that faith and adventure tied to mission and purpose. The Christian church of the first century was not bound in its thinking as we are. Like their forebears, Christians sensed God's purpose among men and thought of themselves as God's people on mission—called, sent, commissioned. They were a covenant people, under the divine mandate to "go make disciples." They met together wherever and whenever they could. Their identity as a people lay in their beliefs, their commitments, and their purpose. I daresay the church of tomorrow will have some of those same characteristics.

Flexibility Needed

For one thing our society requires flexibility. People today are on the move, from city to city, from job to job. They sometimes move en masse from rural areas to the cities. They move on weekends in a mass exodus to recreation areas. Established parish patterns are difficult to hold together, and we feel threatened by this. The old familiar ways feel good. We are comfortable with the customary ways. We are threatened by the revolutionary ideas of going out where the people are. (Who ever heard of a worship service on the lakeshore or in a factory?)

While the radicals and revolutionaries sometimes challenge our accepted theology, they more often challenge our mentality—our frame of thinking. Do we sometimes get the essentials and the nonessentials confused? The central issues and peripheral concerns? This calls for careful thought because, while we must hold fast to basic convictions, we need to be flexible and imaginative in our methods and approaches.

Two things, then, seem imperative: First, to deepen and clarify the knowledge and sense of the saving, redeeming truth. Second, to relax our fearsome grip upon patterns no longer effective. Failure at either point can spell disaster. We are being told that the gospel itself must be allowed to break out from its captivity in our obsolete structures, that the face of Christ is too often hidden or obscured by secondary things, that we take our organizations too seriously and Christ not seriously enough.

This really was the nature of the problem in Jesus' day. He said very little that had not been said before. The problem was that no one was expected to take the teaching seriously: "This people honors me with their lips." Jesus did take it seriously. He *was* what he taught. And they crucified him for it. Are we in danger of crucifying for a similar reason?

What Will the Church Be Like?

What characteristics will the church of tomorrow have? In a time of population explosion and of knowledge explosion, of mobility and automation, of interplanetary travel, what is tomorrow's church to be like if it is to minister effectively? Who can say? At least let us think about it.

First, the church needs to have a continuous, progressive grasp on essential truth. Underscore essential! We cannot, we dare not, major in minors. We dare not cling to what is old but distinguish what is basic. Jesus said, "When the Spirit of truth comes, he will guide you into all the truth." That sounds pretty dynamic and progressive. We are invited to engage in a search and quest. The timeless is always timely. If what we have hold of is eternal in quality, we need not fear that it will be outdated. But we will be driven again and again to seek the deeper understanding. We may be jarred loose from superficial and easy ideas which we recite from the teeth out.

This means that when the volume of knowledge is growing so rapidly and new vocabulary is being written every day, Christians ought to be courageous thinkers. Our young people cannot be asked to put their religious faith in a separate compartment untouched by their understanding of science and philosophy. Nor can they be asked to sacrifice their intellectual integrity.

Jesus placed the premium upon hunger and thirst for righteousness, upon humility, awareness, seeking, growing. He bypassed the know-it-alls and turned to those whose minds were open to wonder, love, and praise. Of those whose minds were closed, preoccupied with their own righteousness, he spoke in heartbreaking tones, "Let them alone." Would he still say that? Frightening, isn't it?

Second, the church of tomorrow will surely be a community of love, strong in fellowship, and an example in human relations. "By this shall all men know that ye are my disciples, if ye have love one to another." God is love. If people are to sense anything about God among us, there will have to be a genuine fellowship of redeeming love.

There is, for countless thousands, no real human relatedness, no security in loving relationships. That is where life is breaking down. Science and technology can give us fabulous products or take us through space but only love can enable us to live together in peace on this earth. The church is the custodian of the very truth and spirit which could create a brotherhood among men. And while it is beyond our reach to do the great and massive thing or suddenly to change humanity as a whole, we have within our reach the possibility of forming a genuine fellowship of love right where we are.

A local congregation can be universal in its outlook and spirit. It can demonstrate eternal values. It can do on a small scale what has the mark of the universal upon it.

And that which has such value will have symbolic meaning far beyond itself. We can live inclusively. We can cross the lines of discrimination. We can reach out to the lost and lonely, the deprived and rejected. We can be a community of redeeming love. There is an element of risk, of course. There always is.

We can be more sensitive to people, to persons one by one, to their suffering, their failures, their needs, and their potential. And this is needed on the part of Christian people as a whole. There are always a few who have deep concerns but if the church is to march into its tomorrows with any real contribution to make, our people need to be taught that to be Christian is to *care* for persons.

Love is more than sentiment. It is intelligent concern, creative insight, redemptive attitudes. How can we learn to be responsive in love to people? The most compelling thing in any congregation is the way people feel about one another and about the person who has lost his way. Evangelism will have to take on more of such meanings rather than a mere platform performance that attempts to be sensational and thus get results.

Third, and hard on the heels of what we have just said, the future church will be a movement among laymen and significant to laymen. The early church was a lay movement. Jesus was a layman! The apostles were laymen too, fishermen whom he made "fishers of men." The church in that day was a phenomenon! You can't account for it in human or rational terms, but certainly one mark was spontaneity among laymen. Christianity to them was a calling, a vocation. Everyone was a minister, a priest, a servant. That is, every Christian served others and shared the new life in Christ.

The form of the church today is not the same as it was in that day when the church was young and vigorous, before it was overorganized and heavy with its own weight.

The mission came first and everyone was involved (before that word was worn threadbare). Perhaps we are beginning again to see how the church ought to be.

One reason why the recently converted person is more effective in winning others is that his experience with the heartbreak of guilt and the bondage of sin is more recent and vivid. He still cares. Perhaps one reason that the layman is more effective in his witness to the non-Christians than the clergyman is that he is closer to where they live and remembers where they hurt. He may also be more spontaneous and natural. There will always be need for the trained professional to teach, to equip, to counsel, to shepherd the people. But it will be the layman who best communicates the Christian heritage to others at the place where they live and work.

Fourth, tomorrow's church will have to let the gospel speak in relevant, vital terms. (It is relevant, of course, if it is not hidden or distorted.) The gospel is power! It is revolutionary in its very nature. It was when the church was small and when it took the gospel seriously that it shook the world. Without property, without ponderous organization, without traditions, ritual or regalia, it was unencumbered and free. Its identity was in its convictions ("Christ is risen!") and its commitments ("into all the world").

Once the church was at the center of the community, but one by one, the several functions of the church have been assumed by others. Charity and benevolence, for instance, have been taken over by the government, by the United Fund. No longer are many funerals conducted from the church building. The funeral parlor has replaced it. No longer is extensive teaching done by the church. The public school does that though some churches continue to make a significant contribution through play schools and child care relieving working mothers and through well-done Sunday schools. A change in form and function is taking place and we seek effective ways to relate to pressing needs now. This is a challenge! The gospel is indeed relevant.

Fifth, it is at the point of the central faith and witness that the church has her very life. Jesus said, "You shall be witnesses unto me." The Holy Spirit bears witness to his words and makes them "known." It is this vital truth and its realization in human life that is the church's primary business. Certainly there are ramifications in social as well as individual life but here is the church's heart and soul.

The church is always within one generation of extinction. It is alarming to see how very little young people of the church know about the Bible and the heroes of the faith. They know all about movie and television stars. They can tell you about the outstanding athletes and their records. They know these things because they have constant exposure to them. But in matters of the Christian faith many young people who have gone to church all their lives are virtually illiterate. If we don't do a better job of teaching our youth, there will be no church of tomorrow.

Sixth, the church of tomorrow will have to know a spiritual power very often lacking. We are very activistic. "The lights are on at our church every night of the week," one pastor said proudly. But the church is called to be holy before it is called to hum. Our very activism may be a cover-up for the spiritual poverty we feel.

John R. Mott once said that we have multiplied Christian activities faster than we have developed Christian life and experience to sustain them. We need more people who will live habitually at close quarters with God and in warm fellowship with his children. We are indeed called to *do,* but we are first called to *be.*

"Mystical," cries the cynic. All right, we need a revival of the sense of God, the experiential relationship with him. We cannot have greater fruitage until we have greater rootage. Only the Holy Spirit can illuminate the mind, kindle the heart, and stir the will to obedience. "Not by might, not by power, but by my spirit saith the Lord." This is not refuge in other worldliness either (or shouldn't be). It is to train and empower us for our neighbor's need.

Two things stood out very clear in Jesus of Nazareth. He lived in unbroken unity with God, and he lived for other people, not for himself. Study again his three great temptations in the wilderness at the beginning of his ministry. They concerned the *how* of saving the world. Out of the mystical came the practical. Out of sensitivity to God came sensitivity to people.

The church of tomorrow will have to be responsive—imaginative, alert, seeking, growing, dynamic. That's the kind of world we live in. God is at work in his world.

TALK BACK

1. Of the congregations you know, how many would you consider progressive and vital? How would you rate your own congregation—on a percentage scale?

2. On what basis would you evaluate progressiveness? What would be the measuring stick? (If we don't know, is it possible that right there is part of our problem?)

3. How much danger is there that the church will lose its real identity and witness in times like these? How can it be strengthened and made *more* vital in its witness?

Study Activity

Try to draw up a projection for your congregation and its ministry in your community over the next ten years—as a business or industry would project plans for expansion and service. Share your findings with your pastor and others.

---

[1]Gilbert W. Stafford, "The Movemental Nature of the Church," *Vital Christianity* (Sept. 22, 1968), pp. 14-15.

Chapter 13

Workers Together— With God!

M y Father has worked [even] until now. — He has never ceased working. He is still working—and I too must be at [divine] work" (John 5:17, Ampl.). So said Jesus when he was severely criticized for healing on the Sabbath day. Not only did he assert that God was still active in the world but also that he was giving priority to human beings rather than rigid rules. The second letter to the Corinthians (6:1) boldly claims that Christians are God's fellow workers in his purpose of reconciling people to the Father and to one another. The apostle sensed this companionship. Now, if God continues his creative and redemptive work in the world, how can we sense what he is doing and work with him?

As early as 1961 Dr. Charles Malik, distinguished Lebanese statesman and significant Christian, said: "We are really at the end of a whole epoch of history, and we do not know what the new epoch is going to be."[1] Then he raised three questions: (1) What is this new thing being born? (2) Where is Christ in it? (3) What is our role, both severally and collectively, in its formation? He reminded me of the Apostle Paul, who wrote to the Romans in the first century A.D., "The night is far spent, the day is at hand: let us therefore cast off the works of darkness, and let us put on the armor of light" (13:12). Both Paul and

121

Dr. Malik sensed that the times were changing, something new was on the horizon. History bears out Paul's claim, and it is bearing out Malik's claim. What is it that is being born?

Christian leaders, in a sense, should be like good journalists. They should be able to see what is emerging, to interpret the times, and to sense what is needed. The prophets were like that, and their words speak with meaning even today. God is a living God. You are never quite prepared for the things he has in store. He works through the social process, at the point of interaction between and among individuals and groups, but he works most through dedicated, sensitive persons. There are many points of conflict and interaction where there is only blind hostility and selfish purpose. God can't get in, because no one is listening to him.

The idea on the other hand that social disorder and unrest are totally evil is an error. These times *can* be fertile soil for Christian action and witness. The church was born under conditions of unrest. Practically all new creative movements arise out of unrest. What can come out of the unrest today? Anything? It depends on whether we Christians relate helpfully to it. What is the new thing being born and where is God at work in it?

What Is God About These Days?

The New Testament is set in the framework of *hope*. The hope of Israel was the belief that the Messiah, the anointed one, would come. They were a called people, under covenant with God, anticipating the fulfillment of the promise. Christians in the New Testament were also a called people. "I . . . beseech you," wrote Paul, "that ye walk worthy of the vocation wherewith ye are called . . . Ye are called in one hope of your calling" (Eph. 4:1, 4).

There was an ongoingness about this. In the time of

stress and tension, there was both *calling* and *hope*. That makes the difference. Christians are people with hope in their hearts. Can we, then, with insight upon developing trends, with dedication to act courageously, and with hope in our hearts, discern what God is about in these days? Let us make some attempt.

First, on the global scale, there is rising in many countries a vigorous nationalism and the shaking off of old, colonial shackles. There is a kind of grass roots protest at controls from outside the country and an insistent demand for the right to shape their own destiny. With the rise of nationalistic spirit there is frequently a rejuvenation of the religion and culture established in that land. Missionary work long established by "sending" churches in Europe and America is sometimes threatened. Even the national (indigenous) church leaders, imbibing of the nationalistic spirit, want quickly to throw off all controls from outside. These countries are very often under the leadership of angry men in a hurry. Often they lack the competence and experience so important for such leadership. So, being insecure, they may be hostile to all outside influences—even to the missionary work of the church which has been associated in their minds with colonialism.

But look beyond now. The very spirit of independence may speed up the development of a strong, indigeneous church if we have the wisdom and patience to release responsibility properly and establish a relationship of mutual respect as sister churches. Is God at work? Very likely we will look back upon these times of testing and see where he has indeed been at work. Missionary Boards are changing policy. In country after country, the church grows stronger as the mission staffs are reduced to the specialized services where they are most needed.

Second, in the deep loneliness of our time mentioned

in the first chapter, the hunger and need has inspired wholesome developments. There has been a groundswell of small, face-to-face groups which has proved to be a tremendous blessing to many churches. Impersonal and formal worship which leaves people cold and relatively unmoved is supplemented—in some cases counteracted—by such small groups of six to twelve or fifteen people who meet for study, spiritual quest, discussion of their problems, and intercessory prayer.

Some sizable interdenominational movements have arisen, involving quest groups and retreats. These have proved to be very significant in the lives of thousands of Christian people and have simply transcended in spirit denominational differences among them. New meanings concerning the nature of Christian fellowship and of the church have been realized as "two or three" come together in a life-sharing relationship in Christ. This fellowship—koinonia—is the essential nature of the church. It is not difficult to see the hand of God at work there.

Third, despite resistance to heavy ecclesiastical structures in organized Christianity, there are signs of new life and vitality in the church. In the last decade or two there has been more emphasis on the ministry of every person than ever before, perhaps, since the days of the early church. In this, we have begun to recapture something of the spirit of that dynamic young church. Even the practice of footwashing which had been written off by the majority of the Christian leaders has come to be seen in a different light, as symbolic of one of the deepest meanings of the Christian life. Christians are to be servants, like their Lord.

Many pastors see their work in a new light—as equippers and teachers. Read Ephesians 4:11-12 again to see that is just what the pastor's work was in that day. Pastors, too, are reacting against the ponderous church machinery and are increasingly concerned about getting to the business of helping people. They are weary of "baby-sitting" with people who should have grown up years ago. They are weary of the demands of petulent and self-centered church members who never really do anything for anybody.

There is a new awareness of persons as persons, of the conditions under which they have to live, and of the influences which tend to rob them of their worth as persons. We are exchanging our plate glass mirror in which we have seen ourselves for a plate glass window through which we look out to see life about us. Some have ventured to go out where people live and suffer. Others are trying to muster up the courage.

Part of this going out is taking the form of "occupational groups." A ministry is being taken to people where they labor. Some clergymen doff their clerical garb and put on working clothes, identifying more with people. Some have chosen specialized ministries such as the chaplaincy in an institution or in the military service; some have become industrial chaplains working within the structure of some industry. These and other forms of ministry have met with increasing favor. As a matter of fact some congregations are finding it difficult to secure qualified leadership. Perhaps the truth is dawning upon us, and the church is becoming more outgoing.

Fourth, in the very complexity of life today and in the massive nature of social problems, Christians are being forced to new concerns for Christian unity. They must unite in order to make any impression or bear any notable witness. "We wrestle not against flesh and blood, but against principalities, against powers, against the rulers of the darkness of this world, against spiritual wickedness in high places" (Eph. 6:12). The pressures which pull the world apart could have the effect of pulling Christians together if we react in a Christian way.

Our time calls for Christian statesmanship—or *worldsmanship*. (If there is no such word, there ought to be.) The ability to see long range, to sense the deeper meanings, to perceive what God's will is for today and tomorrow—these are qualities the church needs, especially in its leaders. The trouble is that we hear mostly the voices of those on the outer fringes—revolutionaries and reactionaries on the "left" and "right." The great body of Christian people remain silent, for the most part, and inactive. Much depends upon whether these can be aroused and challenged to effective action. The future of any church depends upon whether its membership can be mobilized for continuous evangelism. A new mood, a new conviction is needed. Strangely enough, the thing called for is just what we see in the New Testament church: a deep sense of mission under God, a keen concern for people, a warm and loving fellowship, a spontaneous participation by laymen (nonprofessionals), the sense of divine guidance, and a hope that can see beyond the immediate things to what God is doing.

A New Formula

Someone has come up with the "Three Rs"—reading righting, and reconciliation. Reading to become informed. Righting the wrongs. Reconciling man to God and man to man. Three very essential ingredients for an effective and redemptive church. Look at them.

First, reading is the way most of us can become widely informed and aware. First-hand experience in any area is most vivid and real but we are necessarily limited in the amount of that we can acquire. Furthermore, there are few who can reflect helpfully upon that experience and gain a deeper sense of its meaning. Gifted people, however, who have wide experience and ability to interpret it, have most frequently shared in writing.

In these days when so much entertainment comes right into our homes, we tend to come to the surface in our thinking and draw only superficial conclusions. We have a vast wealth of information at our fingertips in any good library, and in a steady stream of literature coming off the press each year. Christians ought to care enough to inform themselves and to be aware of more than the passing parade of events which remain unrelated and without interpretation in their minds. Reading widely and wisely is our best preparation for intelligent action.

Second, righting the wrongs that exist around us is something within our reach. If a person has been mistreated because his skin is a different color, an act of courtesy and respect is the best antidote. If the laws of your city or state are unfair to some of its citizens, who cares enough to take action? If landlords refuse to maintain decent quarters for their tenants or charge them unreasonable rent, they ought to be exposed. The people who suffer most are least able to bring any influence to bear. The church as a body has some responsibility!

Third, reconciling is at the heart of Christianity. Our Lord came to reconcile man to God and to his fellowman. That is our ministry too. The individual Christian has a responsibility to become a reconciler, to build bridges of understanding, to create confidence, and to make peace as well as to lead other people to Christ. The local congregation has the responsibility of becoming a community of love, a fellowship of reconciliation.

The New Testament says very little about forms and methods. Jesus largely ignored mere rules and demonstrated love. "Love thy neighbor," said our Lord again and again. When a lawyer tried to sidestep its meaning and asked, "Who is my neighbor?" he told of the Samaritan who crossed over the lines of nationalistic pride and bigotry to help a fellow human being. It really wasn't a difficult or involved question at all. It was simply a question of whether he would obey the clear command of love.

Can a congregation become a fellowship of love and reconciliation? Can we inform ourselves about conditions around us and marshal our forces to secure justice and opportunity for those who are trapped by prejudice and discrimination or by economic forces over which they have no control? Can we become reconcilers in the true sense of that word, bringing people to the living Christ? We can't do everything now but we can do something now.

The church will come alive when we begin to obey. It will be renewed when it is centered again upon its mission. Our fellowship will have new quality when we open it outward, living and loving inclusively.

TALK BACK

1. Where do you see God working today? Of the areas suggested in this chapter, which if any do you think might be valid? Analyze the suggestions.

2. List the rapid or revolutionary changes taking place. Do you see where good might come of some?

3. What do you think of the "Three Rs" idea? How do you evaluate this as a realistic and effective approach?

Study Activity

Bring a number of newspapers or newsmagazines to the study group. Divide into small work groups of four or five people. Look for: big world problems, personal catastrophes, great unresolved issues. Mark or clip these. Rate these according to their importance and discuss what the church can do now and across the next few years to help meet these situations.

---

[1]Charles Malik, "The Gospel and the Life of the Spirit," *The Christian Century* (Aug. 23, 1961).